THE APPLE COOKBOOK

BY

CHARLOTTE POPESCU

CAVALIER COOKBOOKS

An imprint of Cavalier Paperbacks

Published by Cavalier Cookbooks 1997
Reprinted 1999
Reprinted 2002
Reprinted 2004
Reprinted 2007
Reprinted 2009
Reprinted 2014

An imprint of Cavalier Paperbacks
Burnham House,
Upavon,
Wilts SN9 6DU

Cover illustration by Beverley Lees

ISBN 978 1 899470 44 0

Printed by CPI Group (UK) Ltd, Croydon, CR0 4YY

CONTENTS

INTRODUCTION

The apple is Britain's national fruit and there are over 2,000 varieties. Apples and apple orchards are part of our cultural heritage and have been around since Roman times. The apple is a dominant fruit in myths and folklore. Apples were the fruit on the Tree of Knowledge in the Garden of Eden. Magical apples grew on King Arthur's Isle of Avalon. In myths and poetry it is the golden apple that tempts and which is always just out of reach. In the myth of "Hesperides and the Golden Apples", Hera has received an apple tree of golden apples as a wedding present from the Goddess of the Earth. The Hesperides were sisters who guarded the apples. They were helped by a dragon, Ladon. One of Heracles' twelve labours was to carry off the golden apples which he did by killing the dragon. Apples also feature in the story of Atalanta's race. Atalanta refused to marry until one of her suitors beat her in a race. Milanion succeeded in winning her by dropping three golden apples at intervals. Atalanta stopped to pick them up and lost the race. In poetry beautiful things are likened to apples and apple trees. Rossetti wrote that beauty was "like the sweet apple which reddens upon the topmost bough".

Apples have been used in cooking for centuries and are popular today for their different textures, tastes and many culinary uses. Although there are countless varieties, most supermarkets and grocers still offer only a small selection.

Probably the most popular English eating apple, the Cox's Orange Pippin was raised by Richard Cox in the 1820s. Other easily available eating apples in supermarkets are Granny Smith, Discovery, Fiesta, Spartan, Laxton's Superb, Idared, Royal Gala, Braeburn, and Golden and Red Delicious. Invariably the only cooking apples on sale are Bramley Seedlings. Eating varieties you may have heard of include Egremont Russet, Sturmer Pippin, Worcester Pearmain, Blenheim Orange, Orleans Reinette, Ashmead's Kernel, James Grieve, Ellison's Orange, Tydeman's Early Worcester and Tydeman's Late Orange and other Pippin varieties such as Ribston. They are all delicious in their own way and may well be found in farm shops and local farmers' markets in the autumn.

Unfortunately Britain is losing many apple orchards - roughly a third have disappeared since the 1960s. This book aims to encourage people to cook with apples and maybe, discovering how useful they are, to plant their own apple trees!

NOTES FOR THE COOK

If you have a fan-assisted electric oven reduce the specified heat in the recipes by 10 - 20°C.

1 teaspoon = 5 ml
1 tablespoon = 15ml

SOUPS AND STARTERS

Spicy Apple Broth

Curried Parsnip and Apple Soup

Beautiful Pea Green Soup

Mulligatawny Soup

Colourful Carrot Soup

Caramelised Onion Tart

Goat's Cheese Tartlets

Creamy Pickled Herrings

Apple Curry Sauce

SPICY APPLE BROTH

Serves 2 - 4

25g, 1oz (2 tbsp) butter
1 onion, peeled and chopped
600ml, 1pt (2½ cups) chicken stock
1 level tbsp curry powder
1 tbsp cornflour
2 egg yolks
150ml, ¼pt (²/₃ cup) double cream
2 Cox's or other tart eating apples, peeled and cored
salt and pepper
juice of ½ lemon
watercress leaves

Melt the butter, add the chopped onion and cook until soft, but not brown. Stir in the chicken stock and curry powder and add the cornflour mixed with a little water. Bring to the boil and simmer for 8 minutes. Gently warm the cream and add the egg yolks. Stir this mixture gradually into the hot soup. Remove from heat and transfer the mixture to an electric blender. Slice one of the apples and add to the blender. Blend until smooth, or pass through a fine sieve. Season to taste with salt and pepper. Chill. Dice the remaining apple and marinade in lemon juice to keep its colour. Just before serving, stir in diced apple and garnish the soup with the watercress.

CURRIED PARSNIP
AND APPLE SOUP

Serves 4 - 6

25g, 1oz (2 tbsp) butter
1 tbsp oil
225g, 8oz onions, peeled and chopped
1 tbsp curry powder
450g, 1lb parsnips, peeled and sliced
225g, 8oz cooking apples, peeled, cored and chopped
600ml, 1pt (2½ cups) chicken stock
150ml, ¼pt (²/₃ cup) milk
150ml, ¼pt (²/₃ cup) white wine
salt and pepper
2 crisp eating apples, cored and chopped

Melt the butter and oil in a heavy saucepan and add the chopped onions. Then stir in the curry powder, parsnips and cooking apples. Cook together gently for 10 minutes. Add the stock, milk and wine, bring to the boil and simmer for 30 minutes or until the parsnips are soft. Purée in a food processor or blender. Reheat and, if liked, add the two chopped eating apples just before serving.

BEAUTIFUL PEA GREEN SOUP

Serves 4 - 6

50g, 2oz (4 tbsp) butter
3 onions, peeled and chopped
2 eating apples, cored and chopped
1 tsp curry powder
450g, 1lb peas
1.2litres, 2pt (5 cups) chicken stock
2 handfuls of mint

Fry the onions in the butter in a large saucepan for 5 minutes. Then add the chopped apples. Cook for 2 minutes, then stir in the curry powder. Add the peas and stock. Season with salt and pepper and stir in half the mint. Cover and simmer for 20 minutes. Leave to cool. Add the remaining mint and purée in a food processor or blender until smooth. This soup may be served hot or cold.

MULLIGATAWNY SOUP

Serves 4 - 6

50g, 2oz (¼ cup) butter or margarine
1 onion, peeled and chopped
1 carrot, peeled and chopped
100g, 4oz swede, peeled and chopped
1 eating apple, peeled, cored and chopped
50g, 2oz streaky bacon, chopped
25g, 1oz (¼ cup) flour
1 tbsp curry powder
1 tbsp tomato purée
2 tbsp mango chutney
600ml, 1pt (2½ cups) beef stock
1 tsp mixed herbs
pinch of ground cloves
salt and pepper
50g, 2oz (¼ cup) long grain white rice

Melt the butter in a saucepan, add the onion, carrot, swede, apple and bacon and fry until lightly browned. Stir in the flour, curry powder, tomato purée and chutney and cook gently for 1 minute while continuing to stir. Remove from the heat and gradually stir in the stock, herbs, ground cloves and seasoning. Bring to the boil and cook until thickened. Cover and simmer for 30 minutes. Cool slightly, then sieve or purée in a blender or food processor until smooth. Return the soup to the pan, bring to the boil, add the rice and boil gently for about 10 minutes, stirring occasionally. Serve immediately.

COLOURFUL CARROT SOUP

Serves 2 - 4

100g, 4oz carrots, peeled and sliced
1 handful watercress
1 tin of chopped tomatoes
50g, 2oz cooking apple, cored and chopped
300ml, ½pt (1¼ cups) of water
salt, pepper and sugar

Put all the ingredients into an electric blender or food processor and process until smooth. Add a little salt, pepper and sugar to taste. Serve very cold.

CARAMELISED ONION TART

Serves 6

225g, 8oz puff pastry
100g, 4oz (½ cup) butter
325g, 12oz red onions, peeled and sliced
pinch of nutmeg
sprinkling of black pepper
450g, 1lb cooking apples, peeled, cored and sliced
50g, 2oz (½ cup) brown sugar
150ml, ¼pt (²/₃ cup) Calvados or brandy
Parmesan cheese

Roll the pastry and use to line a greased 20cm (8in) flan dish. Cook the onions in a frying pan using half the butter. Add the nutmeg and pepper. Stir for a minute or two. Remove the onions, and put the apples and brown sugar in the pan with the rest of the butter. Cook for a couple of minutes, and add the Calvados or brandy. Cook for a few more minutes, then remove the apples with a slotted spoon. Boil the Calvados or brandy and butter until the mixture has reduced and becomes sticky. Spread the onion mixture over the pastry, pile the apples on top and cover these with the Calvados or brandy. Bake in the oven at gas mark 6, 200°C (400°F) for 20 minutes.

GOAT'S CHEESE TARTLETS

Makes 8 tartlets

150g, 6oz shortcrust pastry
1 large cooking apple, peeled, cored and sliced
225g, 8oz goat's cheese, sliced

Roll out the pastry and use to line eight greased 5cm (2in) tartlet tins. Arrange 2 or 3 slices of apple in each tartlet. Bake the tartlets in the oven at gas mark 4, 180°C (350°F) for about 15 minutes. Remove from the oven, and put a slice of goat's cheese on top of the apple in each tartlet. Return to the oven and cook for a further 5 minutes to allow the goat's cheese to melt.

CREAMY PICKLED HERRINGS

Serves 4

1 onion, peeled
2 eating apples, peeled and cored
juice of ½ lemon
1 small carton soured cream
salt and pepper
4 pickled herrings

Slice the onion into rings. Cover with boiling water and leave to soak for 2 minutes. Drain and chill. Dice the apples and sprinkle them with lemon juice. Add the onion rings, soured cream and salt and pepper. Mix the ingredients together. Drain the herrings and lie flat. Spoon the apple and onion mixture over the top and serve.

APPLE CURRY SAUCE

This sauce can be served as a party dip with fresh raw vegetables such as carrots cut into matchsticks, cauliflower florets, courgette and celery sticks and cucumber slices. Alternatively it goes well with cold slices of chicken or turkey.

100g, 4oz (1 cup) mayonnaise
2 tbsp cream
1 tbsp mango chutney
2 tbsp curry powder
1 cooking apple, peeled and cored
1 tsp lemon juice
pinch of salt
1 tsp sugar
pinch of ground ginger

Mix together all the ingredients except the apple. Grate or chop the apple finely and mix it into the sauce. Reserve some small cubes of apple to garnish the sauce.

SUPPER DISHES

Creamy Chicken with Cider and Apples

Autumn Chicken

Apple, Chicken and Vegetable Casserole

Orchard Chicken

Easy Cheesy Chicken and Apples

Turkey and Apple Burgers

Crusty Lamb Pie

Spicy Pork Chops

Pork and Cider Casserole

Pungent Pork Fillet

Creamy Pork Fillet

Pork Surprise Parcels

Pheasant Casserole with Cream and Apples

Apples and Trout in Cider

Trout with Lemon and Apples

Apple Stuffed Mackerel

Tasty Gammon Steaks

Apple and Sausage Pasties

Ham, Apple and Potato Bake

Cheesy Bacon and Apple Pie

Sausage and Apple Pie

Rabbit and Cider Casserole

CREAMY CHICKEN WITH CIDER AND APPLES

Serves 6

6 chicken breasts
75g, 3oz (¾ cup) flour
125g, 5oz (²/₃ cup) butter
450g, 1lb cooking apples, peeled, cored and chopped
225g, 8oz onions, peeled and chopped
450ml, ¾pt (1¾ cups) dry cider
180ml, 6fl oz (¾ cup) chicken stock
180ml, 6fl oz (¾ cup) double cream

Dust the chicken breasts with half the flour. Melt half the butter in a frying pan and fry chicken until brown. Place in a casserole. Cook the apples and onions until soft, stir in remaining flour and add cider and stock. Bring this to the boil and pour over the chicken. Cook in the oven at gas mark 4, 180°C (350°F) for 30 minutes. Spoon out the chicken onto a serving plate. Boil the remaining sauce rapidly to reduce it by half. Add cream and remaining butter but do not allow to boil. Pour sauce over the chicken and serve.

AUTUMN CHICKEN

This makes a tasty casserole. Serve with baked potatoes
and carrots.

Serves 4

4 chicken breasts
2 tbsp sunflower oil
2 onions, peeled and chopped
225g, 8oz mushrooms, chopped
1 cooking apple, peeled, cored and chopped
300ml, ½pt (1¼ cups) apple juice
300ml, ½pt (1¼ cups) chicken stock
1 bay leaf
black pepper, freshly ground
parsley
croutons (optional)

Heat the oil in a casserole. Fry the chicken until golden brown.
Remove to a plate. Fry the onions, mushrooms and apple for 5
minutes. Return the chicken to the casserole and add the apple
juice and stock. Add the bay leaf and some freshly ground
black pepper. Cover and cook in the oven at gas mark 4,
180°C (350°F) for 1½ hours. If you want to thicken the sauce,
mix a little cornflour with water and add to the casserole and
cook for a further 5 minutes. Garnish with parsley and croutons.

APPLE, CHICKEN AND
VEGETABLE CASSEROLE

Serves 4

225g, 8oz parsnips
225g, 8oz turnips
225g, 8oz carrots
225g, 8oz swedes
325g, 12oz onion, peeled
2 tbsp olive oil
4 chicken breasts or quarters
100g, 4oz green lentils
2 eating apples, peeled, cored and sliced
200ml, 7fl oz (¾ cup) apple juice
300ml, ½pt (1¼ cups) chicken stock
salt and pepper
parsley

Peel and slice the root vegetables and chop the onions. Heat the oil in a large casserole and add the chicken pieces. Brown well and remove from the pan. Add the vegetables and sauté for 5 minutes. Add the lentils, sliced apples, apple juice and chicken stock and bring to the boil. Season with salt and pepper and replace the chicken. Cover and cook at gas mark 5, 190°C (375°F) for 1 hour. Garnish with parsley and serve.

ORCHARD CHICKEN

Serves 6

6 chicken breasts
2 tbsp oil
chicken stock
25g, 1oz (1 tbsp) plain flour
2 onions, peeled and chopped
1 tsp crushed coriander seeds
¼ tsp cinnamon
¼ tsp powdered saffron
½ tsp ground ginger
450g, 1lb pears, peeled, cored and sliced
225g, 8oz eating apples, peeled, cored and sliced
225g, 8oz plums, halved with stones removed
lemon juice
1 tbsp chopped parsley

Coat the chicken breasts in flour and fry in the oil in a casserole with the chopped onion until crisp and golden all over. Add enough stock to cover the chicken. Mix in the coriander seeds, cinnamon, saffron and ginger. Cover and simmer for 30 minutes. Add the sliced pears, apples and plums to the casserole. Simmer for a further 20 minutes until the chicken is tender. Sharpen to taste with lemon juice. Serve sprinkled with chopped parsley.

EASY CHEESY CHICKEN
AND APPLES

This is a good way of using up left over chicken.

Serves 4

3 cooking apples, peeled, cored and sliced
50g, 2oz (¼ cup) butter
325g, 12oz cooked chicken, sliced
100g, 4oz (1 cup) Cheddar cheese, grated
300ml, ½pt (1¼ cups) white sauce
salt and pepper
pinch of dry mustard
4 tbsp breadcrumbs

Butter an ovenproof dish. Fry the apple slices in the butter. Put the sliced cooked chicken in the dish and lay apple slices on top. Mix half the grated cheese into the white sauce, season with salt, pepper and mustard and pour over the apples. Mix the breadcrumbs with remaining cheese and sprinkle over the sauce. Bake at gas mark 5, 190°C (375°F) for 20 minutes.

TURKEY AND APPLE BURGERS

These are excellent healthy burgers which are a firm favourite
with my children.

Serves 4

325g, 12oz turkey mince
4 spring onions, chopped
1 tsp chopped chives
1 cooking apple, peeled, cored and grated
50g, 2oz (½ cup) fresh breadcrumbs
salt and pepper
1 egg, beaten
sunflower oil
3 tbsp mango chutney

Put the turkey mince in a bowl with the onions, chives, grated
apple, breadcrumbs and salt and pepper. Bind together with
the beaten egg and form into burger shapes. Chill for 30 minutes and then either fry in sunflower oil, or brush with oil and
barbecue over hot coals. Serve in baps with mango chutney.

CRUSTY LAMB PIE

This is an excellent way of using up lamb left over from a
roast.

Serves 6

225g, 8oz shortcrust pastry
325g, 12oz cooked lamb, chopped into cubes
325g, 12oz cooked ham, chopped
1 large cooking apple, peeled, cored and chopped
1 large onion, peeled and chopped
1 tsp rosemary
300ml, ½pt (1¼ cups) chicken stock
300ml, ½pt (1¼ cups) cider

Place the lamb, ham, apple and onion in a 22.5cm (9in) pie
dish, mix well and sprinkle with salt and pepper to taste and
the rosemary. Pour over the stock and cider. Roll the pastry
into a circle and cover the lamb mixture with the pastry lid. Cut
a slit in the pastry and brush with beaten egg or with a little
milk. Bake in the oven at gas mark 4, 180°C (350°F) for 40
minutes.

SPICY PORK CHOPS

Serves 4

4 thick pork chops
75g, 3oz (¾ cup) muscovado sugar
2 tbsp cider vinegar
1 clove of garlic, crushed
1 tsp dry mustard
60ml, 2fl oz (¼ cup) olive oil
60ml, 2fl oz (¼ cup) sherry
50g, 2oz (½ cup) walnuts
2 cooking apples peeled, cored and sliced
25g, 1oz (2 tbsp) butter
salt and pepper
½ tsp ground cinnamon

Marinade the chops in a sauce made with the sugar dissolved in the vinegar and with the mustard and garlic added. Heat oil in a large frying pan. Fry the chops for about 10 minutes on each side until caramelised. Remove the chops and keep warm on a serving plate. Pour sherry into the pan and allow to bubble for 1 minute, then pour over the chops. In another pan melt the butter and toss the walnuts in it. Add the apple slices and fry until golden. Season with salt, pepper and a pinch of cinnamon. Arrange the apple slices and walnuts over the pork chops and serve immediately.

PORK AND CIDER CASSEROLE

A good, hearty casserole for all the family.

Serves 6

900g, 2lb pork fillet
450g, 1lb onions, peeled
4 sticks celery
50g, 2oz (¼ cup) butter
450ml, ¾pt (1¾ cups) cider
4 level tbsp tomato purée
mixed herbs
450g, 1lb cooking apples, peeled, cored and sliced
salt and pepper

Trim and cube the pork. Slice the onions and chop the celery. Gently fry the pork on both sides in the butter until it is brown. Transfer to a casserole. Add the onions to the butter and cook until they are transparent. Add the celery to the onions and turn well in the juices. Place these vegetables in the casserole with the pork. Add the sliced apples and cook gently in the butter for 2 minutes, then add to the casserole with the cider, tomato purée, mixed herbs and salt and pepper. Cook for about 1 hour at gas mark 4, 180°C, 350°F.

PUNGENT PORK FILLET

Rice or new potatoes and French beans would go well with this pork dish. It makes an easy and quick supper party main course.

Serves 4

240ml, 8fl oz (1 cup) cider
325g, 12oz pork fillet
2 tbsp sunflower oil
1 tsp dry mustard
1 clove of garlic, crushed
pinch of ground ginger
50g, 2oz mushrooms, sliced
2 cooking apples, peeled, cored and sliced
6 spring onions, sliced
1 tbsp soya sauce
salt and pepper

Reduce the cider by boiling rapidly. Cut the pork fillet in half lengthways and slice very thinly. Heat the oil in a large frying pan and cook the pork. Sprinkle in the mustard, crushed garlic and ginger. Add the mushrooms and apples. Pour over the soya sauce and the cider and let everything bubble while you continue to stir. Season with salt and pepper. When the juices are syrupy, add the spring onions and cook for another 5 minutes.

CREAMY PORK FILLET

Serves 4

40g, 1½oz (3 tbsp) butter
450g, 1lb pork fillet
1 onion, peeled and sliced
1 cooking apple, peeled, cored and sliced
2 tbsp Calvados or brandy
240ml, 8fl oz (1 cup) chicken stock
60ml, 2fl oz (¼ cup) cream or crème fraîche

Melt most of the butter in a pan and seal the pork fillet on all sides until brown. Remove from the pan, add the remaining butter and cook the onion until soft. Add the apple and cook until golden. Return the pork to the pan with the Calvados or brandy and set alight. Pour over the stock, cover and cook gently for 30 minutes. Remove the pork and keep warm. Stir in the cream and heat gently. Slice the pork fillet and serve with the sauce.

PORK SURPRISE PARCELS

The children will enjoy finding the sliced apple inside these burgers.

Serves 4

225g, 8oz minced pork
1 onion, peeled and finely chopped
pinch of mixed herbs
salt and pepper
1 large egg, beaten
1 cooking apple, peeled, cored and cut into quarters
2 tbsp flour
dried breadcrumbs
oil for frying

Mix together the pork, onion, herbs and seasoning and bind with most of the beaten egg. Flour your hands, take some mixture and wrap around one piece of apple, shaping it into a burger. Repeat this process until you have 4 large burgers. Roll the pork burgers in flour, dip in the rest of the beaten egg and coat with breadcrumbs. Fry in oil until golden brown.

PHEASANT CASSEROLE
WITH CREAM AND APPLES

Serves 4

1 pheasant
2 tbsp olive oil
1 onion, peeled and chopped
4 rashers streaky bacon, chopped
3 eating apples, peeled, cored and sliced
180ml, 6fl oz (¾ cup) dry cider
150ml, ¼pt (²/₃ cup) single cream
salt and pepper

Heat the oil in a casserole. Add the pheasant and brown, turning frequently. Add the onion and chopped bacon and fry gently. Slice the apples and add to the casserole. Add the cider and cover with a lid. Cook over a low heat for about 1 hour, turning the bird halfway through the cooking time. Remove the bird, simmer until almost all the liquid has gone, then stir in the cream and adjust seasoning. Pour over the pheasant and serve.

APPLES AND TROUT
IN CIDER

Serves 4

4 trout, cleaned and gutted with heads and tails removed
1 carrot, peeled and chopped
2 stalks celery, cut into strips
2 onions, peeled and chopped
50g, 2oz (¼ cup) butter
large lettuce leaves
240ml, 8fl oz (1cup) dry cider
3 tbsp crème fraîche
parsley

Sauté the vegetables in some of the butter and place in the cavities of the trout. Dip the lettuce leaves in boiling water for a second or two, cut out central stem and wrap the trout up in the leaves. Place in a buttered baking dish and dot with butter. Pour over the cider and bake at gas mark 6, 200°C (400°F) for about 30 minutes. Remove trout from the sauce, and keep warm. Reduce the sauce by boiling it for a couple of minutes, and stir in the crème fraîche. Pour over the trout and serve garnished with parsley if liked.

TROUT WITH LEMON
AND APPLES

Serves 4

4 large rainbow trout, cleaned and gutted
1 tbsp lemon juice
½ tsp rosemary
50g, 2oz (¼ cup) butter
2 eating apples, cored and thickly sliced
freshly ground black pepper
parsley
lemon wedges

Sprinkle the inside of the trout with pepper, lemon juice and rosemary. Fry the trout in butter over moderate heat for 5 minutes. Turn the fish over, add the apples and cook for a further 6-8 minutes, turning the apples once, until the fish are cooked and the apples are brown. Serve the fish surrounded by the apples, garnished with lemon wedges and parsley.

APPLE STUFFED MACKEREL

Serves 4

4 mackerel, cleaned and gutted with heads removed
75g, 3oz (¹/₃ cup) butter
1 medium onion, peeled and chopped
100g, 4oz white cubed bread
1 large cooking apple, peeled, cored and chopped
1 tbsp chopped parsley
½ tsp dried basil
grated rind of 1 lemon
salt and pepper

Fry the onion in the butter until softened, then add the bread cubes. Mix in the chopped apple and cook until it is soft. Add the herbs, lemon rind, salt and pepper. Stuff the mackerel and secure with cocktail sticks. Place in a greased ovenproof dish and bake in the oven at gas mark 4, 180°C (350°F) for about 40 minutes.

TASTY GAMMON STEAKS

Serves 4

900g, 2lb red cabbage, shredded
2 cooking apples, peeled, cored and sliced
1 bay leaf
several cloves
50g, 2oz ($^1/_3$ cup) caster sugar
2 tbsp vinegar
4 gammon steaks
4 tbsp brown sugar
25g, 1oz (2 tbsp) melted butter

Put the cabbage, apples, bay leaf, 3 or 4 cloves and sugar in a pan with a little water, cover, bring to the boil and simmer for 30 minutes. Brush the gammon steaks with melted butter. Sprinkle with brown sugar and stick in some cloves. Grill for about 8 minutes on each side and serve with the red cabbage.

APPLE AND
SAUSAGE PASTIES

These are a good idea for a children's lunch party.

Serves 8

325g, 12oz shortcrust pastry
450g, 1lb sausages
sunflower oil
325g, 12oz cooking apples, peeled, cored and chopped
25g, 1oz (¼ cup) raisins
juice of ½ lemon
pinch of ground cinnamon
1 egg, beaten

Roll out the pastry and cut into about 8 circles. Skin the sausages and fry in the oil until golden. Mix the apples with the raisins, sprinkle with lemon juice and add cinnamon. Bind with some of the beaten egg. Divide the apple filling between the pastry circles and place a sausage on top. Brush the edges of the pastry with beaten egg and fold over in a half-moon shape. Press edges firmly together. Brush the rest of the egg over pasties and place on a greased baking tray. Make slits in the top of each pasty for the steam to escape. Bake at gas mark 6, 200°C (400°F) for 25 minutes.

HAM, APPLE AND POTATO BAKE

A simple hearty supper dish. Serve with green vegetables - broccoli, spinach or green beans.

Serves 2 - 4

2 onions peeled and sliced
25g, 1oz (2 tbsp) butter
2 cooking apples, peeled, cored and chopped
100g, 4oz ham, cubed
½ tsp mixed herbs
salt and pepper
450g, 1lb potato purée, (potatoes mashed with butter and milk)
50g, 2oz (½ cup) breadcrumbs

To make the filling, gently fry the onions and apples in the butter for 5 minutes. Add the ham, herbs and seasoning. Cover the dish with a thin layer of potato purée, then a layer of the filling and alternate layers ending with a potato layer. Cover with breadcrumbs and dot with extra butter. Bake at gas mark 4, 180°C (350°F) for 30 minutes.

CHEESY BACON AND APPLE PIE

Serves 4

225g, 8oz shortcrust pastry
1 onion, peeled and sliced
1 cooking apple, peeled, cored and sliced
225g, 8oz streaky bacon
1 large slice of bread
50g, 2oz Cheddar cheese, grated
2 tsp ground coriander
½ tsp curry powder
1 tsp mixed herbs
pinch of dry mustard
salt and pepper

Make the filling by mincing onion, apple, bacon and bread. Add the cheese, ground coriander, curry powder, herbs, mustard and salt and pepper. Mix well. Roll the pastry into two rounds and use one round to line a greased 20cm (8in) pie tin. Cover the base with the filling and top with the remaining pastry, sealing well. Brush with beaten egg and bake at gas mark 5, 190°C (375°F) for 40 minutes, or until golden brown.

SAUSAGE AND APPLE PIE

This is similar to the previous recipe but incorporates
sausages and potato.

Serves 6

225g, 8oz (2 cups) self-raising flour
100g, 4oz (½ cup) margarine
1 onion, peeled and grated
225g, 8oz pork sausage-meat
1 tbsp snipped chives
225g, 8oz potatoes, par-boiled and sliced
50g, 2oz streaky bacon, chopped
225g, 8oz cooking apples, peeled, cored and sliced

Make the pastry by rubbing the margarine into the flour with
your fingertips. Add the onion and a little water and bind well
together. Roll out two rounds of pastry, one larger than the
other and use the larger round to line a greased 20cm (8in) pie
dish. Mix together the sausage-meat and chives. Layer the
potatoes, sausage mixture, bacon and apples in the pastry. Use
the smaller round of pastry as a lid, sealing the edges well.
Glaze with a little beaten egg if liked and bake in the oven at
gas mark 6, 200°C (400°F) for about 1 hour.

RABBIT AND
CIDER CASSEROLE

A wholesome casserole but not so suitable for the children.

Serves 6

6 rabbit joints
12 prunes
450ml, ¾pt (1¾ cups) dry cider
450ml, ¾pt (1¾ cups) water
2 onions, peeled and chopped
2 tbsp wholegrain mustard
4 bay leaves
4 tbsp plain flour
2 tbsp sunflower oil
450g, 1lb parsnips, peeled and chopped
1 large can of kidney beans, drained

Marinade the rabbit in the prunes, cider, onions, mustard, bay leaves and the water in a large bowl and leave overnight. Lift the rabbit joints out of the marinade, dry, dust with flour and fry in the oil in a casserole. Pour in the marinade, reserving the prunes and add the parsnips. Bring to the boil and then cover and bake in the oven at gas mark 4, 180°C (350°F) for about 40 minutes. Add the prunes and beans and bake for another 30 minutes.

VEGETABLE SIDE DISHES

Apple and Aubergine Ratatouille
Parsnip, Carrot and Apple Roast
Swede and Apple Purée
Tangy Red Cabbage

APPLE AND AUBERGINE
RATATOUILLE

This variation on a ratatouille goes well with pork.

Serves 6

1 large onion, peeled and sliced
1 red pepper, seeded and sliced
1 aubergine, halved and sliced
2 tbsp olive oil
450g, 1lb cooking apples, peeled, cored and sliced
1 large can of chopped tomatoes
1 small courgette, sliced
salt and pepper
mixed herbs

Put the onion, pepper, aubergine, and apple in a large casserole with the olive oil and cook for 10 minutes with the lid on. Season with salt, pepper and a sprinkling of mixed herbs and add the tomatoes and courgette slices. Cover and cook for another 10 minutes and serve hot.

PARSNIP, CARROT
AND APPLE ROAST

Serves 6

This goes well with a simple meat dish.

4 Granny Smiths or other crisp eating apples, peeled,
cored and chopped
450g, 1lb carrots, peeled and chopped
900g, 2lb parsnips, peeled and chopped
6 tbsp olive oil
4 tsp soft brown sugar
salt and pepper

Mix the carrots and parsnips with the oil, sugar and salt and pepper. Place the chopped apples in a roasting tin and top with the vegetables. Cook in the oven at gas mark 6, 200°C (400°F) for 40 minutes.

SWEDE AND
APPLE PURÉE

Serves 6

This is a simple vegetable dish which goes well with pork or
chicken.

900g, 2lb swedes, peeled and sliced
50g, 2oz (¼ cup) butter
325g, 12oz cooking apples, peeled, cored and sliced
salt and pepper
a pinch of nutmeg
1 tsp sugar
double cream

Boil the swedes until soft and then mash with the butter until
smooth. Cook the apples in a little water until tender and purée
them. Stir into the swede purée. Add salt, pepper, nutmeg and
sugar. A spoonful of double cream may also be added.

TANGY RED CABBAGE

Serves 4

450g, 1lb red cabbage, sliced thinly
1 large cooking apple, peeled, cored and chopped
2 onions, peeled and chopped
1 bulb fennel, chopped
2 rashers bacon, chopped
2 tsp caraway seeds
2 tsp creamed horseradish sauce
300ml, ½pt (1¼ cups) plain yoghurt
salt and pepper

Mix the cabbage, apple, onions, fennel, bacon and caraway seeds together. Stir the horseradish into the yoghurt, season with salt and pepper and spoon over the vegetables. Mix everything together and put into a casserole. Bake in the oven at gas mark 3, 160°C (325°F) for 45 minutes.

SALADS

Apple Coleslaw

Fruity Coleslaw

Apple and Pineapple Salad

Red Cabbage and Apple Salad

Waldorf Salad

Apple and Mushroom Salad

Avocado and Apple Salad

Cheddar Cheese and Apple Salad

Crispy Cauliflower Salad

Salami, Potato and Apple Salad

Chicken and Gruyère Salad

Pasta, Prawn and Apple Salad

APPLE COLESLAW

Serves 6 - 8

2 eating apples, cored and sliced
2 carrots, peeled and grated
225g, 8oz white cabbage finely shredded
½ onion, peeled and grated
2 tbsp mayonnaise
2 tbsp olive oil
1 tbsp white wine vinegar
salt and pepper
1 clove of garlic, crushed

Combine the first four ingredients. Add the mayonnaise and a dressing made by mixing the oil and vinegar together with the salt, pepper and a clove of crushed garlic.

FRUITY COLESLAW

This is a delicious coleslaw to serve as part of a cold buffet or to accompany barbecued meats.

Serves 6 - 8

2 crisp red eating apples, such as Spartan or Discovery,
cored and sliced
2 oranges, peeled
225g, 8oz seedless green and black grapes, halved
225g, 8oz white cabbage, shredded
2 tbsp chopped chives
2 tbsp sunflower seeds
4 tbsp lemon juice
2 tbsp clear honey
3 tbsp olive oil
salt and freshly ground pepper

Make the dressing by mixing together the lemon juice, honey and olive oil and add salt and black pepper. Slice the apples thinly and toss in the dressing. Add orange segments, grapes, cabbage, chopped chives and sunflower seeds and mix together.

APPLE AND
PINEAPPLE SALAD

Serves 4 - 6

2 eating apples, peeled, cored and sliced
½ fresh pineapple
225g, 8oz fresh white cabbage, shredded
2 tbsp mayonnaise
2 tbsp olive oil
1 tbsp white wine vinegar
½ tsp Dijon mustard

Mix together the oil and vinegar and add the mayonnaise and mustard. Pour into a large bowl. Add the fruit and cabbage and toss in the dressing. Chill before serving to allow the flavours to develop.

RED CABBAGE AND APPLE SALAD

Serves 4 - 6

900g, 2lb red cabbage, shredded
3 eating apples, peeled, cored and sliced
1 clove of garlic, crushed
300ml, ½ pt (1¼ cups) sunflower oil
150ml, ¼ pt (²/₃ cup) cider vinegar
4 tbsp yoghurt
salt and pepper

Cook the cabbage for 3 minutes in boiling salted water. Drain and leave to cool. Put the sliced apples in a bowl with the cabbage. Combine the crushed garlic, oil, vinegar, yoghurt, salt and pepper to make the salad dressing. Pour over the cabbage straight away and toss together. Cover the bowl and leave in a cool place for a few hours.

WALDORF SALAD

Serves 4

450g, 1lb eating apples, cored and sliced
juice of ½ lemon
1 tsp sugar
150ml, ¼ pt (²/₃ cup) mayonnaise
1 lettuce
4 sticks of celery, sliced
50g, 2oz (½ cup) walnut pieces

Cover the slices of apple with the lemon juice to prevent them going brown. Add the sugar and some of the mayonnaise and leave to stand for 30 minutes. Place lettuce leaves in a bowl with the celery, walnuts, rest of the mayonnaise and apple mixture and serve at once.

APPLE AND
MUSHROOM SALAD

A simple but healthy salad.

Serves 2 - 4

1 Cox's eating apple, cored, peeled and grated
5 white mushrooms, sliced
juice of ½ lemon
½ tsp French mustard
salt and pepper
½ tsp caster sugar
2 tbsp olive oil
50g, 2oz (½ cup) chopped walnuts

Mix the lemon juice, mustard, salt and pepper, sugar and oil in a basin, then toss in the apple and mushrooms. Serve sprinkled with walnuts.

AVOCADO AND
APPLE SALAD

This is a nutritious and healthy salad.

Serves 4 - 6

4 red eating apples, cored and sliced
1 avocado pear
1 head chicory
225g, 8oz (2 cups) cottage cheese
1 yellow pepper, seeded and chopped
100g, 4oz salted peanuts (optional)
6 tbsp mayonnaise
2 tbsp soft light brown sugar
2 tbsp lemon juice

Put the mayonnaise in a bowl and add the sugar and lemon juice. Add the apples to the dressing. Halve the avocado pear, peel and cut into slices and add to the apples. Arrange the chicory around the edge of a shallow dish. Pile the cottage cheese in the centre and arrange the apple and avocado mixture round it. Scatter the chopped yellow pepper and peanuts over the salad and serve at once.

CHEDDAR CHEESE
AND APPLE SALAD

Serves 2 - 4

2 eating apples, peeled, cored and sliced
225g, 8oz Cheddar cheese, diced
2 pineapple rings, chopped
1 round lettuce
150ml, ¼pt (²/₃ cup) soured cream
3 tbsp milk
1 tsp lemon juice
1 tsp caster sugar
¼ tsp salt

Cover the base of a serving dish with lettuce leaves. Combine the soured cream, milk, lemon juice, sugar and salt. Add the apples, cheese and pineapple to the soured cream mixture. Toss lightly together and spread over the lettuce. Serve straight away as this salad will not keep.

CRISPY
CAULIFLOWER SALAD

This is a filling and very tasty salad. It would go down well as part of a cold buffet lunch.

Serves 4 - 6

3 red-skinned apples, cored and thinly sliced, such as
Laxtons or Royal Galas
2 tbsp lemon juice
1 crisp lettuce, shredded
1 cauliflower, broken into florets
100g, 4oz garlic sausage, cut into strips
300ml, ½pt (1¼ cups) mayonnaise
150ml, ¼pt (²/₃ cup) soured cream
1 tbsp curry powder

Sprinkle the apple slices with lemon juice and place in a large salad bowl with the lettuce, cauliflower and sausage. Blend the mayonnaise, soured cream and curry powder together and pour over the salad just before serving.

SALAMI, POTATO AND APPLE SALAD

Serves 4 - 6

225g, 8oz salami (German peppered salami if possible)
3 Cox's eating apples, cored
900g, 2lb new potatoes, cooked
1 clove of garlic, peeled and crushed
6 tbsp mayonnaise
2 tbsp olive oil (extra virgin if possible)
parsley

Cut the salami into small pieces. Cut the apples into small chunks and do the same with the potatoes. Stir the garlic into the mayonnaise. Mix all the ingredients into the mayonnaise and olive oil. Sprinkle with finely chopped parsley.

CHICKEN AND
GRUYÈRE SALAD

Serves 4 - 6

450g, 1lb cooked chicken
4 sticks celery
100g, 4oz Emmenthal cheese
2 red apples, cored and chopped
100g, 4oz black seedless grapes
200ml, 7fl oz (¾ cup) olive oil
2 tbsp white wine vinegar
4 tbsp soured cream
4 tbsp mayonnaise
salt and pepper
4 tbsp parsley
75g, 3oz (¾ cup) toasted pecan nuts or walnuts

Cut the chicken into cubes. Slice the celery, grate the cheese and halve the grapes. Place all these ingredients with the chopped apples in a large bowl. Combine the olive oil, vinegar, soured cream, mayonnaise, salt and pepper and mix this dressing into the chicken, apples, cheese, celery and grapes. Cover and refrigerate. Just before serving decorate with the parsley and toasted nuts.

PASTA, PRAWN
AND APPLE SALAD

Serves 2 - 4

150g, 6oz pasta shells
150ml, ¼pt (²/₃ cup) apple juice
1 tsp chopped mint
1 tsp white wine vinegar
salt and pepper
225g, 8oz peeled prawns
2 Granny Smiths or other crisp eating apples,
cored and chopped
lettuce leaves

Cook the pasta in boiling salted water as per instructions on the packet. Drain well. Whisk together the apple juice, mint, vinegar and salt and pepper for the dressing. Dry the prawns with kitchen paper. Stir the prawns, chopped apples and pasta into the dressing. Cover and keep cool for a couple of hours. Arrange the lettuce leaves in a bowl and spoon the prawn and apple salad on top.

SAUCES, CHUTNEYS AND RELISHES

Apple, Sage and Onion Sauce

Apple and Maple Sauce

Cranberry and Apple Relish

Apple and Cucumber Relish

Indian Spiced Apple Chutney

Apple, Red Pepper and Date Chutney

Green Tomato Chutney

Pineapple and Apple Chutney

Blackberry Chutney

Spiced Crab-Apples

Apple and Horseradish Cream

APPLE, SAGE AND ONION SAUCE

This sauce is delicious with roast pork or chicken.

½ onion, peeled and chopped
25g, 1oz (2 tbsp) butter
325g, 12oz eating apples, peeled, cored and chopped
1 clove of garlic, peeled and crushed
2 tsp dried sage
juice of ½ lemon
90ml, 3fl oz (¹/₃ cup) water
1 chicken stock cube, crumbled

Fry the onion in the butter. Stir in apples, garlic and sage and fry for a minute. Add the crumbled stock cube, the water and the lemon juice and simmer for 20 minutes. Blend or food process and serve hot.

APPLE AND MAPLE SAUCE

An excellent sauce to serve with roast pork, goose or duck.

4 cooking apples, peeled and cored
2 cloves
1 tbsp white wine vinegar
150ml, ¼pt (²/₃ cup) maple syrup
25g, 1oz (2 tbsp) butter

Cut the apples into chunks and place in a saucepan with the cloves, and with just sufficient water to cover. Cook gently until soft. Remove the cloves and blend or food process until smooth. Return to the heat, stir in the vinegar and maple syrup and beat in the butter. Serve the sauce at once.

CRANBERRY AND APPLE RELISH

This relish goes nicely with cold turkey.

225g, 8oz cranberries, washed
325g, 12oz cooking apples, peeled, cored and sliced
2 tbsp cider vinegar
225g, 8oz (1¹/₃ cups) demerara sugar
½ tsp mixed spice
grated rind of 1 orange

Place the cranberries and apple slices in a large saucepan with the vinegar, sugar, spice and orange rind. Simmer for 20 minutes or until fruit is pulpy, stirring occasionally. Cool, cover and refrigerate for up to one week.

APPLE AND CUCUMBER RELISH

This simple relish goes well with ham or sausages. It is also delicious served with barbecued meats, especially pork. The combination of sugar and hot chilli gives it a wonderful sweet but tangy taste.

1 cooking apple, cored and thinly sliced
½ cucumber, diced
2 tbsp granulated sugar
150ml, ¼pt (²/₃ cup) white wine vinegar
½ green chilli pepper, chopped finely

Put the sugar, vinegar and chilli pepper into a saucepan and heat gently until the sugar dissolves. Add the apple slices and bring to the boil. Boil for a couple of minutes, then add the diced cucumber and cook for 5 more minutes. Serve warm or cold.

INDIAN SPICED APPLE CHUTNEY

Makes about 1kg (2.4lb)

As the name suggests this chutney goes well with any curries.

325g, 12oz cooking apples, peeled, cored and sliced
225g, 8oz onions, peeled and chopped
325g, 12oz (3 cups) soft brown sugar
700ml, 1¼pts (3 cups) malt vinegar
100g, 4oz (²/₃ cup) seedless raisins
2 cloves of garlic, crushed
2 tsp salt
2 tbsp ground ginger
1 tbsp mustard powder
1 tbsp paprika
2 tsp ground coriander

Place all the ingredients in a preserving pan or large saucepan. Bring to the boil, then reduce the heat and simmer gently for about 3 hours, uncovered, stirring occasionally, until no excess liquid remains and the mixture is thick and pulpy. Spoon into jars and seal.

APPLE, RED PEPPER
AND DATE CHUTNEY

Makes about 1kg (2.4lb)

900g, 2lb cooking apples, cored and chopped
2 red peppers, halved, seeded, and sliced
100g, 4oz (1 cup) stoned dates, chopped
2 tsp fresh ginger
2 tsp mixed spice
1 tsp salt
450ml, ¾pt (1¾ cups) malt vinegar
450g, 1lb (4 cups) light muscovado sugar

Put all the ingredients in a large saucepan. Heat slowly until the sugar has dissolved, then bring to the boil. Simmer for 40 minutes, stirring occasionally to prevent the mixture sticking to the bottom of the pan. Pour into jars and seal.

GREEN TOMATO CHUTNEY

Makes about 2kg (4½ lb)

450g, 1lb cooking apples, peeled,
cored and finely chopped
225g, 8oz onions, peeled and chopped
1.4kg, 3lb green tomatoes, sliced
225g, 8oz (1¹/₃ cups) sultanas
225g, 8oz (2 cups) demerara sugar
2 tsp salt
450ml, ¾pt (1¾ cups) malt vinegar
2.5cm, 1in piece of root ginger, grated
½ tsp cayenne pepper
1 tsp mustard powder

Put all the ingredients in a preserving pan. Bring to the boil, reduce the heat and simmer gently for about 2 hours, stirring occasionally, until the ingredients are tender and reduced to a thick consistency. Spoon the chutney into jars and seal.

PINEAPPLE AND APPLE CHUTNEY

Makes about 1kg (2.2lb)

This goes well with ham or other cold meats.

450g, 1lb fresh pineapple, diced
225g, 8oz cooking apples, peeled, cored and chopped
100g, 4oz (²/₃ cup) raisins
150ml, ¼pt (²/₃ cup) white wine vinegar
2 tbsp sugar
½ tsp cinnamon
2 tsp ground ginger
2.5cm, 1in piece of root ginger, grated
½ tsp chilli powder
2 cloves of garlic, crushed
1 tsp salt

Put the vinegar, sugar, cinnamon, two types of ginger, chilli powder, garlic and salt into a large saucepan and bring to the boil. Add the pineapple, chopped apple and raisins. Reduce the heat and simmer for about 1 hour. Stir occasionally to prevent anything sticking to the bottom of the pan. Spoon into jars and seal well.

BLACKBERRY CHUTNEY

Makes about 1.4kg (3lb)

This chutney is really tasty and goes well with ham and other cold meats.

900g, 2lb blackberries
325g, 12oz cooking apples, peeled, cored and sliced
325g, 12oz onions, peeled and sliced
2 tsp mustard seeds
2 tsp ground ginger
½ tsp cayenne pepper
pinch of nutmeg
450ml, ¾pt (1¾ cups) malt vinegar
225g, 8oz (2 cups) dark brown sugar

Put all the ingredients except the sugar in a saucepan and bring slowly to the boil. Cook gently until the fruit and vegetables are soft. This will take about 1 hour. Sieve the mixture and return to the pan with the sugar. Stir over a low heat until the sugar has dissolved and the liquid has been absorbed. Pour into clean jars and seal.

SPICED CRAB-APPLES

Makes about 1kg (2.4lb)

This goes well with pork.

1.4kg, 3lb crab-apples, with stalks removed
450ml, ¾pt (1¾ cups) water
lemon rind
225g, 8oz (1⅓ cups) sugar
180ml, 6fl oz (¾ cups) red wine vinegar
1 cinnamon stick
1-2 cloves
3 peppercorns

Put the crab-apples into a large saucepan or preserving pan with the water and some strips of lemon rind and simmer gently until tender. Remove from the heat and strain, reserving the liquid. Put the sugar and vinegar in a pan and add 300ml, ½pt (1¼cups) of the liquid from the fruit. Tie the spices in a piece of muslin and add to the liquid. Heat gently, stirring until the sugar has dissolved and then bring to the boil and boil for 1 minute. Add the crab-apples and simmer gently for 30 minutes until the syrup has reduced to a coating consistency. Remove the muslin bag. Pour into jars and seal.

APPLE AND
HORSERADISH CREAM

This sauce goes really well with smoked mackerel or trout.

150ml, ¼pt (²/₃ cup) soured cream
1 small onion, peeled and finely chopped
2 eating apples, peeled, cored and finely chopped
1 tbsp creamed horseradish sauce
1 tsp wholegrain mustard
salt and pepper

Mix together the soured cream, onion, apple, horseradish and mustard in a bowl. Add salt and pepper to taste. Store in a covered container in the fridge for not more than two days.

PUDDINGS

There are many different puddings that you can make using apples so this is the main section of my book. I have divided them up into seven categories - Pies and Pastries, Crumbles, Pudding Cakes, Batter Puddings, Creamy Desserts, Ice-Creams and Sorbets and All Sorts of Other Puddings.

The simplest way of cooking apples is to make stewed apple or an apple purée. To do this peel, core and slice some apples, add a little water and about 50g, 2oz ($^1/_3$ cup) sugar to 450g, 1lb of apples. Cook covered until soft. To break up the apples and produce a purée, beat with a wooden spoon, or put them through a sieve. You may need unsweetened purée for a recipe, in which case do not add any sugar.

Pies and Pastries

Basic Apple Pie
Spiced Apple Pie
Apple and Blackberry Pie
Spicy Apple and Orange Pie
Creamy Apple Pie
Apple and Elderberry Pie
Apple and Cranberry Pie
Cheese and Apple Pie
Plum and Apple Pie
Potato Apple Pie
Apple and Walnut Filo Pie
Banbury Apple Pie
Kiddies' Apple Tart
Tarte Tatin
Buttery Apple Tart
Amsterdam Apple Tart
Walnut and Apple Tart
French Apple Flan
Velvety Smooth Apple Flan
Lemony Apple Flan
Apple Treacle Tart
Apple Amber
Apple Bakewell Tart
Redcurrant and Apple Strudel
Date and Apple Strudel
Bavarian Strudel
Apple Streusel
Apple Turnovers
Apple Dumplings

Pastry is used in many of the recipes in this
book. Here are some basic types of pastry.

SHORTCRUST PASTRY

150g, 6oz (1½ cups) plain flour
75g, 3oz (⅓ cup) margarine
water

Cut the margarine into small pieces and rub into the flour until
the mixture resembles fine breadcumbs. Add the water and
bind to a firm dough. This is enough pastry for a 20cm (8in)
flan dish. For a 22.5cm (9in) flan use 200g, 7oz flour to 90g,
3½oz of margarine. For a pie use 225g, 8oz flour to 100g,
4oz margarine.

Here are two versions of sweet pastry - you can use either of
these when the recipes in this book call for sweet pastry. Both
versions would make enough for a 20cm (8in) flan dish. For a
22.5cm (9in) flan dish increase the amount of flour to 200g,
7oz (1¾ cups) and the other ingredients in proportion.

SWEET PASTRY NO 1

150g, 6oz (1½ cups) plain flour
75g, 3oz (⅓ cup) butter or margarine
40g, 1½oz (¼ cup) icing sugar
1 egg yolk
1 tbsp water

Process all the ingredients or rub the margarine into the flour
and icing sugar. Bind together with the egg yolk and water and
knead lightly. Chill for 30 minutes before rolling out.

SWEET PASTRY NO 2

150g, 6oz (1½ cups) plain flour
100g, 4oz (½ cup) butter
25g, 1oz (¼ cup) icing sugar

If you have a food processor, put all the ingredients in together and process until it is like breadcrumbs. Otherwise rub the butter into the flour and icing sugar until you have a crumb-like mixture. Pat out the mixture around the base and sides of the flan dish and chill for an hour before baking.

BASIC APPLE PIE

1 quantity shortcrust pastry

675g, 1½lb cooking apples, peeled, cored and sliced
75g, 3oz (½ cup) sugar

Divide the pastry in half. Roll out each half. Use one half to line a greased 20cm (8in) deep pie dish. Put the sliced apples in the pie dish and sprinkle the sugar over them. Roll out the remaining pastry to make the lid. Dampen the pastry rim with water and cover with the lid. Slit the pie in order to let the steam escape and brush with milk or beaten egg to glaze and dust with caster sugar. Bake in the oven at gas mark 6, 200˚C (400˚F) for 30 minutes.

VARIATIONS ON THE
APPLE PIE THEME

SPICED APPLE PIE

Add ¼ teaspoon of cinnamon, ¼ teaspoon of mixed spice, finely grated rind of ½ lemon, 50g, 2oz (¹/₃ cup) sultanas, and 25g, 1oz (2tbsp) melted butter to the sliced apples and continue as for basic apple pie.

APPLE AND BLACKBERRY PIE

Add 225g, ½lb blackberries which have been simmered for about 5 minutes with 50g, 2oz (¹/₃ cup) sugar to 450g, 1lb apples and sprinkle with 50g, 2oz (¹/₃ cup) of sugar.

SPICY APPLE
AND ORANGE PIE

Mix together 1 tablespoon of plain flour, 4 rounded tablespoons of soft brown sugar, 2 teaspoons of cinnamon, ½ teaspoon of ground cloves, 1 teaspoon of nutmeg, 2 tablespoons raisins and grated rind and juice of 2 oranges (made up to 300ml, ½pt (1¼ cups) with water). Stir this mixture into 675g, 1½lb apples and make up the pie as in the basic apple pie recipe.

CREAMY APPLE PIE

Once you have put the apples and sugar in the pie dish cover with a layer of whipped cream, about 150ml, ¼ pt (²/₃ cup) and then cover with a lid and cook as for basic apple pie recipe.

APPLE AND ELDERBERRY PIE

Add a handful of elderberries to the sliced apples and sugar.

APPLE AND CRANBERRY PIE

Add 225g, ½lb cranberries to 450g, 1lb of apples along with the sugar and a pinch of nutmeg. Add 2 table-spoons of flour to the fruit.

CHEESE AND APPLE PIE

For the filling, use 450g, 1lb of apples and 50g, 2oz (¹/₃ cup) of sugar. Add 75g, 3oz sliced Cheshire cheese, the grated rind of 1 lemon and ½ teaspoon of nutmeg.

PLUM AND APPLE PIE

Add 225g, ½lb of plums to 450g, 1lb of apples. Remove stones from the plums before use. Add sugar to taste.

POTATO APPLE PIE

Potato pastry

450g, 1lb potatoes, peeled and chopped
25g, 1oz (2 tbsp) butter
1 tsp brown sugar
100g, 4oz (1 cup) plain flour

Filling

450g, 1lb cooking apples, peeled, cored and sliced
2 tbsp brown sugar
25g, 1oz (2 tbsp) butter

To make the pastry simmer the potatoes in a little water until tender. Drain and mash mixing in the butter, sugar and flour gradually. Knead the pastry until smooth. Roll out and make two rounds, one slightly larger than the other. Place the smaller round in a 20cm (8in) deep pie dish. Arrange the sliced apples over the base and sprinkle with the sugar. Brush the border of the pastry with water and place the larger round on top, sealing well. Make a small hole in the pastry to allow steam to escape. Bake in the oven at gas mark 6, 200°C (400°F) for about 30 minutes. Remove and cut a little hole in the pastry. Pop the butter inside the pie and fill up the hole again. Cook for a further 5 minutes and then serve at once.

 ## APPLE AND WALNUT FILO PIE

100g, 4oz (½ cup) butter
100g, 4oz (²/₃ cup) caster sugar
grated rind and juice of 1 lemon
1 egg
25g, 1oz (¼ cup) self-raising flour
½ tsp ground cinnamon
675g, 1½lb eating apples, peeled, cored and sliced
275g, 10oz packet filo pastry
50g, 2oz (½ cup) walnuts, chopped and toasted

Beat together 50g, 2oz (¼ cup) butter, 50g, 2oz (¹/₃ cup) caster sugar, grated lemon rind, egg, flour, ¼ teaspoon of cinnamon and the walnuts. Mix apples with remaining 50g, 2oz (¹/₃ cup) caster sugar, a tablespoon of lemon juice and the other ¼ teaspoon of cinnamon. Melt a further 50g, 2oz (¼ cup) of butter and use some to grease a 25cm (10in) flan dish. Line with half the layers of filo pastry, buttering each layer of pastry. Spread nut mixture over pastry base and top with apples. Fold pastry edges over filling and top with more layers of pastry to cover the filling, buttering each layer as before. Bake in the oven at gas mark 5, 190°C (375°F) for about 50 minutes, covering loosely with foil if the pastry browns too much. Serve warm, sprinkled with icing sugar.

BANBURY APPLE PIE

325g, 12oz (3 cups) plain flour
pinch of salt
150g, 6oz (¾ cup) butter
1 tbsp caster sugar
1 egg, beaten
675g, 1½lb cooking apples, peeled and cored
juice of ½ lemon
100g, 4oz (²/₃ cup) sultanas
75g, 3oz (¾ cup) soft brown sugar
pinch of cinnamon
pinch of nutmeg
grated rind and juice of 1 orange

To make the pastry, put the flour and salt in a bowl and rub in the butter until the mixture resembles fine breadcrumbs. Stir in the caster sugar, then stir in the egg and enough water to bind the mixture together. Knead on a lightly floured surface, then roll out two thirds of the pastry and use to line a large greased pie dish. Thinly slice the apples. Put in a bowl and sprinkle with lemon juice. Layer the apples, sultanas, brown sugar, spices and orange rind in the pie dish. Sprinkle with the orange juice. Roll out the remaining pastry to form a lid, pressing the edges together. Make a slit in the centre of the pie. Brush the top with milk to glaze, then bake at gas mark 6, 200˚C (400˚F) for 30 minutes until golden brown. Sprinkle the top with caster sugar and serve hot or cold.

KIDDIES' APPLE TART

This is so quick and easy that you can get the children to
make the filling.

1 quantity shortcrust pastry

Filling

2 cooking apples, peeled and cored
juice of ½ lemon
1 tbsp demerara sugar
1 egg

Roll out the pastry and use to line a greased 20cm (8in) round
flan dish. In a bowl grate the apple and add the lemon juice
immediately to prevent the apple from going brown. Mix in the
sugar and beaten egg. Combine all ingredients thoroughly.
Spoon into the pastry case and cook in the oven at gas mark
4, 180°C (350°F) for 20 minutes.

TARTE TATIN

There are several ways of making this classic tart. Here is one of the simpler versions.

1 quantity sweet pastry

75g, 3oz (¹/₃ cup) butter
175g, 7oz (1¾ cups) muscovado or brown sugar
450g, 1lb cooking apples, peeled, cored and sliced

Spread half the butter on the base of a round pie dish. Sprinkle all over with half the sugar. Lay the slices of apple neatly over the sugary base. Melt the remaining butter and pour over the fruit and sprinkle with remaining sugar. Roll out the pastry and cover the pie. Tuck the edges down between the apples and the edge of the dish. Put in the oven at gas mark 6, 200°C (400°F) for 30 minutes. Turn the tart upside down onto a serving dish. The apples will look caramelised. Serve with cream.

BUTTERY APPLE TART

1 quantity sweet pastry

Filling

4 Granny Smith apples, peeled and cored
lemon juice
100g, 4oz (½ cup) butter
125g, 5oz (1¼ cups) brown sugar
1 tsp cinnamon
½ tsp nutmeg
a few drops vanilla essence
3 eggs

Line a greased 20cm (8in) flan dish with pastry and bake blind in the oven at gas mark 4, 180°C (350°F) for about 20 minutes. Slice the apples, brush with lemon juice and arrange them in the pastry case. Put the butter, sugar, spices and vanilla into a heatproof bowl. Beat the eggs and transfer them to the bowl as well. Place the bowl over a pan of simmering water and stir until the butter melts and the sugar has dissolved. Pour over the apples. Return to the oven and cook for 15-20 minutes until the filling is just firm to touch.

AMSTERDAM APPLE TART

1 quantity sweet pastry

450g, 1lb cooking apples, peeled, cored and grated
grated rind and juice of 1 lemon
50g, 2oz (½ cup) chopped almonds
50g, 2oz ($^1/_3$ cup) sultanas
50g, 2oz ($^1/_3$ cup) caster sugar
2 tbsp raspberry jam

Line a greased 20cm (8in) flan dish with the pastry. Reserve a little pastry. Mix together apples, lemon rind and juice, almonds, sultanas and sugar. Spread raspberry jam over the flan dish and then fill with the apple mixture. Roll out the reserved pastry and make a lattice design over the filling with strips of pastry. Bake in the oven at gas mark 6, 200°C (400°F) for 30 minutes.

WALNUT AND APPLE TART

1 quantity shortcrust pastry

450g, 1lb cooking apples, peeled and cored
150ml, ¼pt (²/₃ cup) whipping cream
100g, 4oz (²/₃ cup) caster sugar
1 egg
75g, 3oz (¾ cup) flour
1 tsp cinnamon
1 tsp vanilla essence
¼ tsp nutmeg
50g, 2oz (½ cup) walnuts

Line a greased 22.5cm (9in) flan dish with the pastry. Slice the apples and transfer to flan dish. Mix together the cream, sugar, egg, flour and seasonings (this can be done in a food processor if you have one). Pour over apple slices and top with the walnuts. Bake at gas mark 4, 180˚C (350˚F) for 40 minutes.

FRENCH APPLE FLAN

1 quantity sweet pastry

Custard

100g, 4oz (²/₃ cup) caster sugar
3 tbsp cornflour
½ tsp vanilla essence
450ml, ¾pt (1¾ cups) milk
4 egg yolks

Topping

675g, 1½lb cooking apples, peeled, cored and sliced
50g, 2oz (¼ cup) butter
50g, 2oz (¹/₃ cup) demerara sugar

Roll out the pastry and use to line a greased 22.5cm (9in) flan dish. Bake the pastry case blind in the oven at gas mark 5, 190°C (375°F) for 15 minutes. Make the custard by putting the sugar in a saucepan with the cornflour and vanilla essence and blend with a little milk. Add the rest of the milk and bring to the boil, stirring all the time until the mixture thickens. Cook for a minute. Remove from the heat and beat in the egg yolks one at a time. Return to the heat and cook gently for 5 minutes, stirring all the time. Do not boil. Turn off the heat and allow to cool before pouring into the pastry shell. Slice the apples and fry in the butter, sprinkled with the sugar. When almost tender arrange on top of the custard in overlapping layers. Serve warm or cold.

VELVETY SMOOTH
APPLE FLAN

This is a good recipe to make if you are making meringues
and have spare egg yolks.

1 quantity shortcrust pastry

450g, 1lb cooking apples, peeled, cored and sliced
2 tbsp water
50g, 2oz (¼ cup) butter
2 tbsp caster sugar
3 digestive biscuits, crushed
grated rind of 1 lemon
2 tbsp brandy
2 tbsp double cream
2 egg yolks
pinch of nutmeg

Line a greased 20cm (8in) flan dish with the pastry and bake
blind in the oven at gas mark 4, 180°C (350°F) for 15 minutes.
Cook the apples with the water until soft. Beat to a purée,
then whisk in the butter and caster sugar, followed by the biscuit crumbs, lemon rind, brandy and a pinch of nutmeg. Whisk
the egg yolks with the cream and stir this into the cooled apple
mixture. Pour into the flan dish and cook for a further 30 minutes.

LEMONY APPLE FLAN

1 quantity sweet pastry no 2

3 eggs
75g, 3oz (½ cup) caster sugar
150ml, ¼pt (²/₃ cup) single cream
grated rind and juice of 2 lemons
450g, 1lb cooking apples, peeled and cored
icing sugar

Roll out the pastry and use to line a greased 22.5cm (9in) flan dish. Chill for 30 minutes. Prick the pastry base and bake blind at gas mark 4, 180°C (350°F) for about 15 minutes. Place the eggs, cream and the caster sugar in a bowl and whisk together. Add the grated lemon rind and lemon juice and whisk until smooth. Grate the apples into the lemon mixture and spoon into the pastry case. Return to the oven and bake for about 40 minutes or until set and golden brown. Dust with icing sugar.

APPLE TREACLE TART

1 quantity shortcrust pastry

2 eggs
150ml, ¼pt (²/₃ cup) whipping cream
1 cooking apple, peeled, cored and grated
6 tbsp golden syrup
50g, 2oz (½ cup) brown breadcrumbs
rind and juice of ½ lemon

Roll out the pastry and use to line a greased 20cm (8in) flan dish. Beat the eggs and whisk in the cream. Add the grated apple, golden syrup, breadcrumbs, lemon rind and juice and mix well together. Pour over the pastry case and bake in the oven at gas mark 4, 180°C (350°F) for about 25 minutes.

APPLE AMBER

1 quantity shortcrust pastry

Filling

675g, 1½ lb cooking apples, peeled, cored and sliced
50g, 2oz (¼ cup) butter
rind and juice of 1 lemon
50g, 2oz (½ cup) brown sugar
2 egg yolks

Meringue

2 egg whites
100g , 4oz (²/₃ cup) caster sugar

Line a greased 20cm (8in) flan dish with the pastry. Cook the apples with the butter, lemon juice and sugar gently until tender. Stir to break up, add the egg yolks and lemon rind and beat well. Pour this mixture into the pastry case and bake at gas mark 5, 190°C (375°F) for about 30 minutes. Meanwhile whip the egg whites until stiff and fold in the sugar, a little at a time to make sure all is well incorporated. Spoon meringue mixture over the apples and return to a cool oven for a further 20-30 minutes, by which time the meringue should be golden brown.

APPLE BAKEWELL TART

1 quantity shortcrust pastry

2-3 tbsp apple marmalade or blackberry and apple jelly
(see page 179 or 175)
100g, 4oz (½ cup) margarine
100g, 4oz (²/₃ cup) caster sugar
100g, 4oz (1 cup) ground almonds
1 egg, beaten

Roll out the pastry and use to line a greased 20cm (8in) flan dish, prick well and spread the jam over the base. To make the filling melt the margarine in a pan and add the sugar, ground almonds and beaten egg. Pour the filling over the jam. Bake in the oven at gas mark 6, 200°C (400°F) for about 30 minutes. Remove from the oven and allow to cool before serving.

REDCURRANT AND
APPLE STRUDEL

225g, 8oz puff pastry
4 large cooking apples, peeled, cored and sliced
2 tbsp soft brown sugar
1 tsp vanilla essence
100g, 4oz (½ cup) butter
4 tbsp breadcrumbs
2 tbsp redcurrant jelly
50g, 2oz (½ cup) chopped almonds
icing sugar

Sprinkle the apple slices with brown sugar and add vanilla. Roll the pastry as thinly as possible on a well floured tea-towel into a rectangle. Melt 50g, 2oz (¼ cup) of the butter in a pan and fry the breadcrumbs until golden. Melt the rest of the butter and spread over the pastry. Sprinkle the breadcrumbs over the pastry, spreading the apples over the top. Dot with the redcurrant jelly and the almonds. Fold in the edges of the pastry and roll up like a swiss roll. Place the strudel on a buttered baking tin and brush again with melted butter. Bake in the oven at gas mark 4, 180°C (375°F) for about 45 minutes, brushing with butter every so often. Dust with icing sugar and serve with cream.

DATE AND APPLE STRUDEL

225g, 8oz puff pastry
225g, 8oz cooking apples, peeled, cored and sliced
2 tbsp lemon juice
50g, 2oz (1/3 cup) demerara sugar
50g, 2oz (½ cup) breadcrumbs
50g, 2oz (½ cup) ground almonds
100g, 4oz (1 cup) stoned dates, chopped
25g, 1oz (¼ cup) flaked almonds
2 tbsp caster sugar

Mix the apples with the lemon juice, sugar, breadcrumbs, almonds and dates. Roll out the pastry on a floured circle into a rectangle. Spoon the apple mixture into the middle of the rectangle. Brush the pastry with a little milk and fold the edges over the apple to enclose it completely. Place on a greased baking tray, seam side down, brush with milk, and sprinkle with sugar and the flaked almonds. Cook in the oven at gas mark 5, 190°C (375°F) for 30 minutes. Serve cut into slices with whipped cream.

BAVARIAN STRUDEL

In this strudel you make your own pastry, rather than using
ready-made puff pastry.

Pastry

100g, 4oz (½ cup) butter or margarine
150g, 6oz (1½ cups) flour
50g, 2oz (¹/₃ cup) sugar
3 tbsp milk

Filling

675g, 1½lb cooking apples, peeled, cored and sliced
25g, 1oz (¼ cup) sultanas
½ tsp mixed spice
75g, 3oz (½ cup) caster sugar
a handful of breadcrumbs
milk and sugar for glazing

Rub the fat into the flour. Add sugar and bind with milk. Knead
a little to make a smooth dough. Mix the sliced apples with
sultanas, spice and sugar. Add the breadcrumbs. Roll out the
pastry on a floured surface into a long strip. Place on a greased
baking tray. Put the apple mixture down the middle. Fold over
the sides of the pastry towards the middle. Brush over with
milk and dust with sugar. Bake in the oven at gas mark 4,
180°C (350°F) for 30 minutes.

APPLE STREUSEL

This is one of my favourite apple puddings - it is a cross
between a pie and a tart.

1 quantity shortcrust pastry

Filling

900g, 2lb cooking apples, peeled, cored and sliced
50g, 2oz (¹/₃ cup) raisins
100g, 4oz (1 cup) plain flour
100g, 4oz (²/₃ cup) caster sugar
50g, 2oz (¼ cup) butter
150ml, ¼ pt (²/₃ cup) double cream

Topping

50g, 2oz (¹/₃ cup) caster sugar
2 tsp cinnamon

Roll out the pastry and use to line a greased 20cm (8in) pie
dish. Make the filling by mixing the apples and raisins together
(if you don't like raisins, these can be omitted). Stir together
the flour and sugar and rub in the butter using your fingertips.
Sprinkle half this mixture over the pastry. Place the apples and
raisins on top and pour over the cream. Spoon over the remaining rubbed-in mixture and sprinkle with the topping of sugar
and cinnamon. Bake in the oven at gas mark 6, 200°C (400°F)
for 40 minutes, reducing the heat if the pie is getting too brown
on top.

APPLE TURNOVERS

1 quantity shortcrust pastry

450g, 1lb apples, peeled, cored and sliced
15g, ½oz (1 tbsp) butter
25g, 1oz (¼ cup) sultanas
grated rind of ½ lemon
50g, 2oz (½ cup) brown sugar

Put the sliced apples, butter, sultanas, lemon rind and sugar in a saucepan and cook for about 5 minutes. Roll out the pastry and cut into large rings, about 12.5cm (5in) in diameter. Put a dollop of apple mixture into each one. Wrap the pastry around the apple and press pastry together firmly. Brush the pastry with milk and dust with caster sugar. Place on greased baking trays. Cook in the oven at gas mark 4, 180°C (350°F) for 20 minutes.

APPLE DUMPLINGS

1 quantity shortcrust pastry

6 cooking apples, peeled and cored
100g, 4oz (1 cup) brown sugar
40g, 1½oz (3 tbsp) butter
12 cloves (optional)

Make the pastry and divide into six portions. Roll each into a round large enough to cover apples. Place an apple on each pastry round, press cloves into each apple, then fill core space with sugar and top with butter. Moisten pastry edges, bring pastry round the apple to cover completely and seal. Place on a baking sheet with pastry join underneath. Brush with milk, dredge with sugar and bake at gas mark 6, 200°C (400°F) for 45 minutes.

Crumbles

Basic Apple Crumble

Apple and Pear Crumble

Apple and Raspberry Scrumble

Apple Mincemeat Crumble

German Apple Pudding

Apple and Rhubarb Crumble

Apple and Blackcurrant Crumble

Apple and Fig Crumble

Apple and Cardamom Crumble

There are lots of ways of doing crumbles. Here are a few suggestions. Each crumble topping can be interchanged with the fillings.

BASIC APPLE CRUMBLE

Filling

675g, 1½lb cooking apples, peeled, cored and sliced
75g, 3oz (½ cup) sugar

Crumble

150g, 6oz (1½ cup) plain flour
75g, 3oz (¼ cup) butter or margarine
50g, 2oz ($^1/_3$ cup) demerara sugar

Put the sliced apple in an ovenproof dish with sugar. Add margarine to flour and rub it in until the mixture resembles breadcrumbs. Then stir in the demerara sugar. Spoon over the fruit and bake in the oven at gas mark 4, 180°C (350°F) for 30 minutes or until the top is brown and the fruit tender.

APPLE AND PEAR CRUMBLE

Use 325g, ¾lb of pears and 325g, ¾lb of apples. Continue as in the basic apple crumble.

APPLE AND
RASPBERRY SCRUMBLE

Filling

450g, 1lb cooking apples, peeled, cored and sliced
225g, 8oz raspberries
100g, 4oz (²/₃ cup) caster sugar
3 tbsp water

Crumble

50g, 2oz (½ cup) plain flour
50g, 2oz (1 cup) porridge oats
50g, 2oz (½ cup) ground almonds
75g, 3oz (¹/₃ cup) margarine
50g, 2oz (¹/₃ cup) brown sugar

Put the sliced apple in a pie dish with the raspberries, caster sugar and water. Put the flour and oats in a bowl with the ground almonds. Add the margarine and rub with the fingertips until the mixture resembles breadcrumbs. Stir in the brown sugar. Pile the crumble mixture on top of the fruit. Bake in the oven at gas mark 4, 180°C (350°F) for 30 minutes until the crumble topping is golden brown.

APPLE MINCEMEAT CRUMBLE

This is a crumble with a difference because it also has a pastry bottom.

1 quantity shortcrust pastry

Filling

450g, 1lb eating apples, peeled, cored and sliced
25g, 1oz (¼ cup) soft brown sugar
225g, 8oz (1 cup) mincemeat

Crumble

50g, 2oz (½ cup) flour
1 tsp cinnamon
50g, 2oz (¼ cup) butter
100g, 4oz (1 cup) soft brown sugar
25g, 1oz (¼ cup) chopped almonds

Roll out the pastry and line a greased 20cm (8in) pie plate. Add the sugar and mincemeat to the sliced apples. Make the crumble by combining the flour and cinnamon. Add the butter and rub in with fingertips. Stir in the sugar and the almonds. Prick the pastry case and bake blind in the oven at gas mark 4, 180°C (350°F) for 15 minutes. Put the apple and mincemeat filling into the pastry case and sprinkle the crumble over the apple mixture to completely cover it. Bake in the oven for a further 35 minutes.

GERMAN APPLE PUDDING

This pudding is also a crumble with a pastry bottom.

100g, 4oz (1 cup) self-raising flour
50g, 2oz (½ cup) brown sugar
25g, 1oz (¼ cup) ground almonds
75g, 3oz (¹/₃ cup) butter
1 tsp lemon juice
1 egg yolk

Filling

450g, 1lb cooking apples, peeled and cored
75g, 3oz (¾ cup) brown sugar
grated rind of 1 lemon
1 tsp lemon juice

Crumble

50g, 2oz (½ cup) plain flour
50g, 2oz (¼ cup) butter
125g, 5oz (1¼ cup) brown sugar
1 tsp cinnamon

Grease a 20cm (8in) cake tin. Mix together the flour, sugar, ground almonds, butter, egg and lemon juice, (this can be done in a food processor of you have one). Put the mixture into the tin. Slice the apples and mix with the brown sugar and lemon rind and juice. Arrange over the pastry. Make the crumble topping by rubbing the butter into the flour. Then stir in the sugar and cinnamon. Sprinkle over the apple and bake in the oven at gas mark 4, 180°C (350°F) for about 1 hour. Serve hot or cold.

APPLE AND RHUBARB CRUMBLE

225g, 8oz cooking apples, peeled, cored and chopped
225g, 8oz rhubarb, chopped
125g, 5oz (¾ cup) sugar

Put the fruit in a pie dish with the sugar. There is no need to pre-cook the fruit. Use one of the crumble toppings from the previous recipes.

APPLE AND BLACKCURRANT CRUMBLE

Filling

325g, 12oz cooking apples, peeled, cored and sliced
325g, 12oz blackcurrants
2 tbsp water
100g, 4oz (²/₃ cup) sugar

Crumble

125g, 5oz (1¼ cups) wholemeal flour
75g, 3oz (¹/₃ cup) margarine
1 tbsp toasted sesame seeds
50g, 2oz (¹/₃ cup) demerara sugar
1 tsp cinnamon

Cook the apples and blackcurrants over a gentle heat with the water and sugar. Turn into an ovenproof dish. To prepare the crumble, rub the margarine into the flour, then stir in the sesame seeds, sugar and cinnamon. Spoon the topping over the fruit and bake at gas mark 5, 190°C (375°F) for 30 minutes.

APPLE AND FIG CRUMBLE

Filling

900g, 2lb cooking apples, peeled, cored and chopped
100g, 4oz no-soak figs, chopped
grated rind and juice of 1 orange
1 tsp ground mixed spice
75g, 3oz (½ cup) sugar

Crumble

150g, 6oz (1½ cups) plain flour
75g, 3oz (¾ cup) soft brown sugar
100g, 4oz (½ cup) butter
50g, 2oz walnut pieces, chopped

Mix the apples and figs with the orange rind and juice, mixed spice and caster sugar. Cook gently, covered, for about 10 minutes. Spoon into a large pie dish and cool. Mix the flour and sugar and rub in the butter. Stir in the chopped walnuts and sprinkle over the apple mixture. Cook at gas mark 4, 180°C (250°F) for 30 minutes.

APPLE AND CARDAMOM CRUMBLE

Filling

675g, 1½lb cooking apples, peeled cored and sliced
75g, 3oz (½ cup) sugar
6-8 cardamom pods

Crumble

150g, 6oz (1½ cups) flour
75g, 3oz ($^{1}/_{3}$ cup) butter
50g, 2oz ($^{1}/_{3}$cup) caster sugar

Prepare the apples as you would for a basic crumble. Take between 6-8 cardamom pods - extract the seeds and lightly crush them with a pestle and mortar. Add to the apples. Make the crumble by rubbing the butter in with the flour and adding the sugar. Place on top of the apples and pat down. This makes a fine crumble not unlike shortbread.

Pudding Cakes

Apple Fudge Pudding

Almond and Apple Pudding

Norwegian Apple Cake

Caramelly Cake

Eve's Pudding

Fudgy Apple and Cream Cheese Cake

Gingery Apple Cake

APPLE FUDGE PUDDING

This is a delicious pudding. It's lovely and gooey and needs to be served with cream or crème fraîche.

Sponge

125g, 5oz (1¼ cups) plain flour
1 tsp baking powder
2 tbsp caster sugar
50g, 2oz (¼ cup) butter or margarine
1 large egg
½ tsp vanilla essence
90ml, 3fl oz (¹/₃ cup) milk

Topping

450g, 1lb cooking apples, peeled and cored
50g, 2oz (¼ cup) butter
150g, 6oz (1½ cups) dark brown or muscovado sugar
1 tsp cinnamon

To make the sponge, mix together the flour, baking powder and sugar. Rub in the butter or margarine with your fingertips as though you are making pastry until the mixture is like breadcrumbs. Whisk the egg and vanilla essence together and add the milk. Stir into the flour and butter mixture and transfer the batter to a buttered rectangular ovenproof dish measuring about 25 x 20cm (10 by 8in). Slice the apples and arrange them on top of the sponge mixture. Lastly, melt the butter, stir in the brown sugar and cinnamon and pour over the apples. Bake in the oven at gas mark 7, 220°C (425°F) for 20 - 25 minutes.

ALMOND AND APPLE PUDDING

This is one of the tastiest versions of an apple pudding with almonds.

450g, 1lb cooking apples, peeled, cored and sliced
3 tbsp honey
2 tbsp water
50g, 2oz (½ cup) breadcrumbs
100g, 4oz (²/₃ cup) caster sugar
50g, 2oz (½ cup) ground almonds
1 egg, beaten
75g, 3oz (¹/₃ cup) butter, melted

Put the apples, honey and water into a pan and cook until the fruit is soft. Stir in the breadcrumbs and place in a shallow ovenproof dish. Put the sugar, ground almonds and egg in a bowl and pour on the melted butter. Mix well and spread over the apple mixture. Bake at gas mark 5, 190°C (375°F) for 45 minutes or a little longer if the almond topping is not set. Serve hot with cream or crème fraîche.

NORWEGIAN APPLE CAKE

This almond and apple pudding is similar to the previous recipe but uses more eggs and includes lemon.

4 large cooking apples, peeled, cored and sliced
75g, 3oz (¾ cup) brown sugar
juice of 1 lemon
sprinkling of cinnamon
100g, 4oz (½ cup) butter
100g, 4oz (²/₃ cup) caster sugar
3 eggs, separated
100g, 4oz (1 cup) ground almonds

Put sliced apples into a buttered round 20cm (8in) baking dish and sprinkle with brown sugar, lemon juice and cinnamon. Cream the butter and caster sugar together until light and fluffy and add the egg yolks, one at a time, beating hard after each addition. Add the ground almonds and mix well. Whisk the egg whites until stiff and fold into the ground almond mixture. Spread this cake topping over the apples and bake in the oven at gas mark 6, 200°C (400°F) for about 30 minutes.

CARAMELLY CAKE

This is a rather special cake. It takes a bit of effort to make but would be suitable as a party dessert.

Topping

butter
3 tbsp caster sugar
450g, 1lb cooking apples, peeled, cored and sliced

Sponge

150g, 6oz (1½ cups) self-raising flour
90ml, 3fl oz (¹/₃ cup) sunflower oil
90ml, 3fl oz (¹/₃ cup) water
60ml, 2fl oz (¼ cup) milk
1 tsp vanilla essence
150g, 6oz (1 cup) caster sugar
2 egg whites

Sauce

2 tbsp water
50g, 2oz (¹/₃ cup) caster sugar
2 egg yolks
4 tbsp single cream
2 tbsp lemon juice

Butter a 20cm (8in) deep cake tin spreading butter thickly over the base. Sprinkle some of the sugar over the butter. Place apple slices all over the butter and sugar and sprinkle more sugar over the slices. To make the cake add the oil, water, milk and vanilla essence to the flour and beat to a thick, smooth batter. Whisk the egg whites until stiff and then whisk in the caster sugar a bit at a time. Fold this mixture into the batter and pour on top of the apple. Cook in the oven at gas mark 4, 180°C (350°F) for 45 minutes. Leave to cool in the tin, then turn out upside down on to a plate.

To make the sauce dissolve 2 tablespoons of water in the sugar over a low heat. Then bring to the boil and allow to bubble until pale golden brown. Remove from the heat and stir in the single cream and then the egg yolks. Return to a low heat for a moment to thicken the sauce and stir in the lemon juice. Spread the sauce over the cake and eat while still warm with extra cream if liked.

EVE'S PUDDING

This is a classic apple sponge.

450g, 1lb cooking apples, peeled, cored and sliced
50g, 2oz (¹/₃ cup) demerara sugar
rind and juice of 1 lemon
75g, 3oz (¹/₃ cup) margarine
75g, 3oz (½ cup) caster sugar
1 egg, beaten
100g, 4oz (1 cup) self-raising flour
a little milk

Grease a round 900ml (1½pt) ovenproof dish. Place the apple slices in the bottom of the dish. Sprinkle the sugar, lemon rind and juice and 1 tablespoon of water over them. Beat the margarine with the sugar until light and fluffy, then gradually beat in the egg, beating well after each addition. Fold in the flour lightly with a metal spoon, adding a little milk if necessary, to give a soft consistency that drops easily from the spoon. Spread over the apples and bake for about 40 minutes in the oven at gas mark 4, 180°C (350°F) until the sponge is set.

FUDGY APPLE AND CREAM CHEESE CAKE

This is a solid but moist cake and is very filling.

Sponge

300ml, ½pt (1¼ cups) apple purée
150g, 6oz (1½ cups) brown sugar
150ml, ¼pt (²/₃ cup) sunflower oil
2 eggs, beaten
225g, 8oz (2 cups) self-raising flour
1 tsp cinnamon
1 tsp ground ginger

Filling

75g, 3oz (¹/₃ cup) cream cheese
75g, 3oz (¹/₃ cup) butter
150g, 6oz (1½ cups) icing sugar
1 tsp vanilla essence

Mix the apple purée with the brown sugar, the oil and eggs. Sieve in the flour, cinnamon and ginger and mix well. Butter two 17.5cm (7in) cake tins. Divide the mixture evenly between the two tins and bake in the oven at gas mark 4, 180°C (350°F) for 30 minutes. Cool slightly in the tins and then turn on to a wire rack. To make the filling beat together the cream cheese, butter, icing sugar and vanilla essence. Use the filling to sandwich the two cakes together. Dust the finished cake with icing sugar.

GINGERY APPLE CAKE

In this recipe slices of apple are incorporated into the sponge.

75g, 3oz (½ cup) caster sugar
75g, 3oz (¾ cup) soft brown sugar
100g, 4oz (½ cup) butter
225g, 8oz (2 cups) plain flour
2 tsp baking powder
1 tsp cinnamon
1 tsp ground ginger
2 eggs
2 tbsp milk
225g, 8oz cooking apples, peeled, cored and sliced
2 pieces of stem ginger (optional)

Cream the sugars with the butter until soft. Sift the flour with the baking powder and spices. Gradually beat the eggs into the creamed mixture then fold in the sieved flour and the milk. Stir in the apple slices and stem ginger. Turn the mixture into a greased deep 22.5cm (9in) cake tin and bake at gas mark 5, 190°C (375°F) for 30 minutes. Serve warm with cream.

Batter Puddings

Apple Batter Pudding

Apple and Pear Clafoutis

Apple Pancakes

Apple Drop Scones

Apple Fritters

APPLE BATTER
PUDDING

Children love this pudding.

Batter

100g, 4oz (1 cup) plain flour
1 egg, beaten
240ml, 8fl oz (1 cup) milk

Filling

25g, 1oz (2 tbsp) butter
450g, 1lb cooking apples, peeled, cored and sliced
50g, 2oz (¹/₃ cup) sugar
grated rind of ½ lemon

First make the batter. If you have a food processor pour in the milk, then the egg and lastly the flour and process until smooth. If not, sift the flour into a bowl, make a well in the centre and add the egg, the milk and gradually work in the flour. Beat until smooth. Next put the butter into a 27.5 x 17.5cm (11 x7in) baking tin and heat in a hot oven at gas mark 7, 220°C (425°F) for a few minutes. Arrange the sliced apples on the base of the tin. Sprinkle with the sugar and lemon rind. Pour the batter over the top and bake for 30 minutes until brown and risen. Serve with golden syrup.

APPLE AND PEAR CLAFOUTIS

This is similar to the Apple Batter Pudding but, with the additon of brandy, is more suited to adults. Clafoutis is a traditional batter pudding made with fruit. Here I have combined apples and pears.

Filling

2 eating apples, peeled, cored and sliced
2 pears, peeled, cored and sliced

Batter

3 eggs
50g, 2oz (½ cup) flour
1 tbsp brandy
50g, 2oz (¹/₃ cup) caster sugar
600ml, 1pt (2½ cups) hot milk
25g, 1oz (2 tbsp) butter
a sprinkling of demerara sugar

Grease a 22.5cm (9in) deep round ovenproof dish and arrange the apple and pear slices in the bottom of it. To prepare the batter beat together the eggs and sugar, stir in the flour, brandy and the hot milk. Beat with a wooden spoon and when you have a smooth batter pour over the fruit and bake in the oven at gas mark 6, 200°C (400°F) for 30 minutes. After about 15 minutes add small pieces of butter to the top of the batter. When cooked remove from the oven and sprinkle with demerara sugar. Serve with cream or, if you have a sweet tooth, with maple syrup.

APPLE PANCAKES

Makes 8 pancakes

Batter

300ml, ½ pt (1¼ cups) milk
1 egg, beaten
100g, 4oz (1 cup) plain flour

Apple filling

450g, 1lb cooking apples, cored, peeled and sliced
25g, 1oz (2 tbsp) butter
50g, 2oz (¹/₃ cup) sugar
1 tbsp lemon juice
½ tsp cinnamon
maple syrup

You can make up the pancake mixture in a food processor. Put the milk in first, then the egg and lastly the flour and process until smooth. If you do not have a food processor, sift the flour into a bowl, make a well in the centre, add the egg and the milk and gradually draw the flour into the liquid, mixing well together until smooth. Fry the pancakes - this mixture should be enough for about eight pancakes. Make the apple filling by melting the butter in a saucepan, add the sliced apples, sugar, lemon juice and cinnamon and cook for about 10 minutes. Do not allow the apples to break up. Divide the apple mixture among the pancakes and roll up. Drizzle with maple syrup and serve.

APPLE DROP SCONES

Makes 8 drop scones

Batter

150g, 6oz (1½ cups) plain flour
1 tsp bicarbonate of soda
25g, 1oz (1 tbsp) caster sugar
1 egg, beaten
240ml, 8fl oz (1 cup) milk
25g, 1oz butter, melted
1 Cox's eating apple, peeled, cored and grated

Maple syrup sauce

120ml, 4 fl oz (⅓ cup) maple syrup
60ml, 2 fl oz (¼ cup) thick single cream
50g, 2oz (¼ cup) butter

Sift together the flour and bicarbonate of soda. Mix in the sugar. Add the beaten egg, milk and melted butter. Stir in the grated apple. Drop the batter into the frying pan in small circles about 7.5cm (3in) in diameter. Turn each drop scone once. To make the sauce, heat the maple syrup, cream and butter gently in a small saucepan. Stir the mixture every so often and simmer for about 10 minutes by which time the sauce will have thickened. Pour over the drop scones and serve straight away.

APPLE FRITTERS

Makes about 12 fritters

These are quick and easy and children will love them.

75g, 3oz (¾ cup) plain flour
pinch of salt
1 egg, separated
1 tbsp oil
2 tbsp milk
2 tbsp water
3 medium sized cooking apples, peeled, cored and cut
into rings
oil for frying
caster sugar

Sift the flour and salt and make a well in the centre. Drop the egg yolk into this. Add the oil and gradually pour in the milk and water stirring the dry ingredients into the egg and liquid. Cover and leave for at least 30 minutes. Whisk the egg white until stiff and fold into the batter. Dust the apple rings with flour as this helps the batter to cling to them, coat with the batter and fry in batches for about five minutes, turning once. Dry on kitchen paper, sprinkle with caster sugar and serve.

Creamy Desserts

Apple Mousse

Apple Snow

Apple Fool

Yoghurt and Apple Whip

Danish Apple Cake

Crunchy Apple and Cinnamon Pudding

Crème Fraîche Apple Crunch

Apple Brûlée

Apple and Toffee Crunch

Creamy Apple Ring

APPLE MOUSSE

900g, 2lb Cox's eating apples, peeled, cored and
chopped
25g, 1oz (2 tbsp) butter
6 tbsp lemon juice
75g, 3oz (¾ cup) brown sugar
15g, ½oz gelatine or vege-gel (the vegetarian
equivalent)
300ml, ½ pt (1¼ cups) double cream
2 egg whites

Cook the chopped apples in the butter and 3 tablespoons of
the lemon juice in a saucepan with the lid on. As soon as the
apple is tender, mix in the brown sugar and beat until puréed.
Remove from the heat. Dissolve the gelatine or vege-gel in 3
tablespoons of lemon juice and add to the apple purée. Allow
to cool. Whip the cream lightly and whisk the egg whites until
stiff enough to stand in peaks. Fold the cream into the apple
purée, fold in the egg whites and leave to set for several hours
in a cool place.

APPLE SNOW

450g, 1lb cooking apples, peeled, cored and sliced
2 tbsp lemon juice
50g, 2oz (¹/₃ cup) sugar
2 egg whites
whipped cream

Cook the apples with lemon juice and sugar in a saucepan until very soft. Beat until puréed or rub through a sieve and leave to cool. Whisk the egg whites until stiff. Fold into the apple purée. Serve in individual glasses or in a bowl topped with cream.

APPLE FOOL

This is a very easy pudding which is useful if you are short of time.

450g, 1lb sweetened apple purée
150ml, ¼pt (²/₃ cup) ready-made custard
150ml, ¼pt (²/₃ cup) double cream
lemon juice

Fold the purée into the custard. Whip the cream and fold this in too. Add a few drops of lemon juice and sprinkle with extra sugar to taste. Turn into one big dish or several ramekin dishes and chill.

YOGHURT AND APPLE WHIP

450g, 1lb cooking apples, peeled, cored and chopped
25g, 1oz (1 tbsp) caster sugar
grated rind and juice of 1 lemon
1 large carton natural yoghurt
2 egg whites

Put apples, sugar, lemon rind and juice in a saucepan and simmer until apple is soft. Beat to a purée and cool. Stir in the yoghurt. Whisk the egg whites and gently fold them into the purée. Pour into a glass dish and serve with light biscuits or brandy snaps.

DANISH APPLE CAKE

This is a quick and easy dish to make and is really tasty.

900g, 2lb cooking apples, peeled, cored and sliced
50g, 2oz (¼ cup) butter
150g, 6oz (1½ cups) brown breadcrumbs
50g, 2oz (½ cup) soft brown sugar
200ml, 7fl oz (¾ cup) whipped cream

Cook the apples in 3-4 tablespoons of water until soft. Beat to a purée. Melt the butter in a frying pan, add the breadcrumbs and sugar and cook until crisp and brown, turning all the time. Turn out onto a plate and leave to cool. Layer the apple purée and breadcrumbs, finishing with a layer of breadcrumbs. Spread the whipped cream over the top, and serve.

CRUNCHY APPLE AND
CINNAMON PUDDING

This is similar to Danish Apple Cake but there are layers of
cream and yoghurt added.

225g, 8oz (2 cups) fresh brown breadcrumbs
3 tsp cinnamon
75g, 3oz (¾ cup) dark brown sugar
75g, 3oz (¹/₃ cup) butter
240ml, 8fl oz (1 cup) whipping cream
25g, 1oz (1 tbsp) caster sugar
1 small carton natural yoghurt
300ml, ½ pt (1¼ cups) apple purée

Mix the breadcrumbs, cinnamon and brown sugar together in
a bowl. Melt the butter in a frying pan and fry the breadcrumb
mixture over a high heat, turning all the time with a wooden
spoon until the mixture is crisp. Leave to cool on a plate. Whip
the cream, whisk in the sugar and stir in the yoghurt. Make
layers of toasted crumbs, apple purée and cream mixture ending with a layer of crumbs. Keep cool until ready to serve.

CRÈME FRAÎCHE APPLE CRUNCH

100g, 4oz (²/₃ cup) caster sugar
150ml, ¼pt (²/₃ cup) water
5 medium sized cooking apples, peeled and cored
300ml, ½pt (1¼ cups) crème fraîche
50g, 2oz (½ cup) brown sugar
6 gingernut biscuits, crushed
25g, 1oz (¼ cup) flaked almonds

Make a syrup with the caster sugar and water. Slice the apples and poach in the syrup for five minutes. Do not allow them to break up. Put the apple slices in a bowl and mix in the crème fraîche and 25g, 1oz (¼ cup) brown sugar. Spoon into a heatproof dish. Mix the biscuit crumbs with the almonds and remaining brown sugar. Sprinkle over the apple mixture and brown under a hot grill. Serve warm or cold.

APPLE BRÛLÉE

This is a quick and simple way to use up apple purée.

300ml, ½pt (1¼ cups) sweetened apple purée
150ml, ¼pt (²/₃ cup) whipped cream
demerara sugar

Divide the apple purée up into several ramekin dishes. Cover with whipped cream and sprinkle with enough demerara sugar to cover the whipped cream. Brown until bubbling under a hot grill and eat either while still warm or allow to cool so that the sugar forms a hard crust over the cream and apple.

APPLE AND TOFFEE CRUNCH

A simple pudding to make which children will love.

450ml, ¾pt (1¾ cups) sweetened apple purée
300ml, ½pt (1¼ cups) whipping cream
1 tbsp golden syrup
50g, 2oz (¼ cup) butter
25g, 1oz (1 tbsp) sugar
100g, 4oz (2 cups) bran flakes, lightly crushed

Spread the purée over the bottom of a serving dish. Whip the cream and spoon over the apple. Melt together the butter and golden syrup, add the sugar and the bran flakes. Mix together well and scatter over the cream. Chill and serve.

CREAMY APPLE RING

3 cooking apples, peeled, cored and sliced
3 tbsp of water
rind and juice of 1 lemon
20g, ¾oz gelatine or vege gel (the vegetarian equivalent)
2 eggs and 2 extra yolks
50g, 2oz (¹/₃ cup) caster sugar
1 small carton cream, whipped

Sauce

75g, 3oz (½ cup) sugar
150ml, ¼pt (²/₃ cup) water
1 tbsp fresh mint

Cook apples with lemon rind and water until tender and beat to a purée. Cool. Soften gelatine or vege-gel in lemon juice and add to the apple mixture. Place eggs, egg yolks and sugar in a bowl and whisk over a pan of simmering water. Stir in cooled apple. Fold in the cream. Turn into a ring mould and chill until set. Turn out and serve with sweet mint sauce. To make the sauce, place all ingredients together and stir over a low heat until the sugar has dissolved. Boil until you have a light syrup. Strain to remove the mint leaves and serve.

Ice-Creams and Sorbets

Apple Ice-Cream

Apple Butter Ice-Cream

Apple and Rum Ice-Cream

Apple and Blackcurrant Ice-Cream

Apple and Walnut Ice-Cream

Applescotch

Pear Ice-Cream

Chestnut and Apple Meringue Ice-Cream

Apple Sorbet

Apple and Ginger Sorbet

Cider Sorbet

Contrary to what many people think, ice-creams are very easy to make without an ice-cream maker. Here are a few ideas for when you have a surplus of apples.

APPLE ICE-CREAM

325g, 12oz cooking apples, peeled, cored and chopped
50g, 2oz (¼ cup) unsalted butter
75g, 3oz (½ cup) sugar
½ tsp ground ginger
2 eggs, separated
150ml, ¼pt (²/₃ cup) single cream
150ml, ¼pt (²/₃ cup) double cream

Put the apples, butter and a little water into a saucepan, cover and simmer until the apples are soft. Beat to a purée. Add sugar and ginger, and then the egg yolks. Beat well and cool. Whisk the creams together and fold into the fruit mixture. Pour into a container and freeze for 1½ hours. Take out of the freezer, whisk egg whites and fold into the mixture. Return to freezer and freeze until firm.

APPLE BUTTER ICE-CREAM

300ml, ½pt (1¼ cups) apple purée
1 tbsp lemon juice
50g, 2oz (¼ cup) softened butter
75g, 3oz (¾ cup) brown sugar
300ml, ½pt (1¼ cups) plain yoghurt
150ml, ¼pt (²/₃ cup) whipped cream

Cut up the butter and whisk it into the apple purée with the lemon juice. Whisk in the sugar, stir in the yoghurt and freeze for about 1 hour. Take out of the freezer, whisk the mixture to help remove ice-crystals and fold in the whipped cream. Return to the freezer and freeze until firm.

APPLE AND RUM ICE-CREAM

This ice-cream is simple and easy to prepare.

600ml, 1pt (2½ cups) apple purée
3 tbsp honey
300ml, ½ pt (1¼ cups) whipped cream
2 tbsp rum or brandy

Mix the honey into the apple purée. Fold the cream whipped up with the rum or brandy into the apple purée. Pour into an ice-cream container and freeze for 1 hour. Take out and whisk the mixture and then put in back in the freezer for at least 4 hours.

APPLE AND BLACKCURRANT ICE-CREAM

This is an easy ice-cream to make and does not need to be taken out of the freezer and beaten at hourly intervals.

225g, 8oz cooking apples, peeled, cored and chopped
225g, 8oz blackcurrants
2 tbsp granulated sugar
4 tbsp water
4 eggs, separated
100g, 4oz ($^2/_3$ cup) caster sugar
300ml, ½pt (1¼ cups) cream, whipped

Combine the apples, blackcurrants, granulated sugar and water and simmer for 15 minutes. Purée mixture in a food processor and then sieve to remove the blackcurrant pips. Whisk the egg whites and whisk in the caster sugar. Whisk the egg yolks until thick and creamy. Fold the fruit purée into the whipped cream and fold into the egg yolks. Lastly fold in the egg whites. Pour into an ice-cream container and freeze until firm.

APPLE AND WALNUT
ICE-CREAM

450g, 1lb eating apples, peeled, cored and sliced
50g, 2oz (¼ cup) unsalted butter
2 tbsp orange juice
25g, 1oz (¼ cup) caster sugar
2 eggs, separated
300ml, ½pt (1¼ cup) double cream
50g, 2oz (½ cup) walnuts, chopped

Cook the apples gently in a covered saucepan with the butter and orange juice until soft. Add the sugar and beat to a purée. Whisk the egg yolks until light and frothy and stir into the purée. Cook over a low heat, stirring, until the mixture thickens slightly. Pour into a bowl and leave to cool. Whisk the cream until thick and fold into the purée with the walnuts. Turn into a freezer container, cover and freeze for about 1 hour. Whisk the egg whites until stiff and carefully fold into the ice-cream. Return to the freezer and freeze until firm.

APPLESCOTCH

450g, 1lb cooking apples, peeled, cored and chopped
50g, 2oz (¼ cup) butter
grated rind of 1 lemon
3 eggs, separated
6 tbsp whisky
300ml, ½pt (1¼ cups) whipping cream
150g, 6oz (1 cup) caster sugar
large crisp eating apples and some lemon juice

Cook the apples with the butter and lemon rind. When soft, beat to a purée. Stir in the egg yolks and cook gently until the mixture thickens. Beat in the whisky and allow to cool. Whip the cream and fold into the apple purée together with half the sugar. Freeze the mixture for 1 hour by which time ice crystals will have formed around the edge. Whisk the egg whites until stiff and whisk in the remaining sugar. Fold into the half-frozen apple mixture. Return to the freezer. You can either serve this ice-cream straight from the freezer or for a dinner party you could hollow out large eating apples and fill with the ice-cream. First cut a thin slice from the stalk end. Carefully hollow out the centre apple flesh and core. Brush the apple with lemon juice. Spoon the ice-cream into the apple and top with apple lids. Freeze until required although you need to remove the apples from the freezer 30 minutes before serving.

PEAR ICE-CREAM

This ice-cream and the following one use apple juice rather than apples.

450g, 1lb pears, peeled, cored and sliced
90ml, 3fl oz (¹/₃ cup) apple juice
75g, 3oz (¾ cup) light brown sugar
¼ tsp cinnamon
2 eggs, separated
150g, 6oz (²/₃ cup) cream cheese, beaten

Poach the pears in the apple juice with the sugar and cinnamon until tender. Purée the pears and pass through a sieve. Then stir the egg yolks into the pear purée and heat gently until a little thicker. Beat the cheese into the pear mixture. Pour into a freezer container and freeze for about 1 hour. Take it out of the freezer, beat it and fold in egg whites that you have whisked until stiff in a separate bowl. Return to the freezer and freeze until firm.

CHESTNUT AND APPLE
MERINGUE ICE-CREAM

1 large can sweetened chestnut purée
150ml, ¼pt (²/₃ cup) apple juice
150ml, ¼pt (²/₃ cup) whipping cream
2 egg whites
50g, 2oz broken meringues

Whisk the apple juice into the chestnut purée until smooth.
Pour into a container and freeze until just becoming firm. Remove from the freezer. Whip the cream and fold in to the half
frozen mixture. Whisk the egg whites and carefully fold them in
as well. Lastly fold in the meringues. Freeze until firm.

APPLE SORBET

3 Granny Smith apples
50g, 2oz (¹/₃ cup) granulated sugar
3 tsp lemon juice
60ml, 2fl oz (¼ cup) water

Core and quarter the apples leaving the skin on (this gives the sorbet a lovely colour). Freeze on a tray, leaving a little space between each. Dissolve the sugar with the water and simmer for 5 minutes. Leave to cool. Defrost the apples slightly and place in a food processor with the sugar syrup and lemon juice. Process until quite smooth, then pass through a nylon sieve to remove the remainder of the skins. Put in a container and freeze for about 2 hours until the edges are frozen but the centre is still mushy. Whisk until smooth then return to the freezer.

APPLE AND GINGER SORBET

450g, 1lb cooking apples, peeled, cored and sliced
grated rind and juice of ½ lemon
3 tbsp soft brown sugar
1 tsp ground ginger
4 pieces of stem ginger, diced
4 tbsp ginger syrup (from the stem ginger jar)
150ml, ¼pt (²/₃ cup) apple juice
2 egg whites

Cook the apples with the lemon rind and juice until very soft. Beat to a purée and stir in the sugar and ginger. Leave to cool. Stir in the stem ginger, ginger syrup and apple juice. Pour into a freezer container, cover and freeze for about 1 hour until mushy. Take out and beat until smooth. Whisk the egg whites until stiff and fold into the apple mixture. Freeze until firm.

CIDER SORBET

150ml, ¼pt (²/₃ cup) dry cider
200g, 7oz (1¼ cup) sugar
200ml, 7fl oz (¾ cup) water
75ml, 3fl oz (¹/₃ cup) lemon juice
500ml, 18fl oz (2 cups) apple purée

Dissolve the sugar in the water. Bring to the boil and boil for about a minute. Strain in the lemon juice and leave to cool. Blend the apple purée and cider into the syrup. Pour into a freezer container and freeze until firm, beating well three times at intervals of about an hour.

All Sorts of Other Puddings

The following puddings in this section are difficult to categorise but here are lots of ideas for all those lovely apples!

Apple Abernethy
Polenta Crumble Cake
Apple Charlotte
Apple Christmas Pudding
Gooey Apple Gingerbread
Apple and Lemon Surprise Pudding
Apple and Orange Pudding
Oat and Apple Pudding
Apple Cobbler
Apple and Blackberry Autumn Pudding
Chocolate and Apple Dessert
Damson and Apple Omelette
Apple Profiteroles
Apple Soufflé
Baked Apples
Apple Meringues
Golden Apple Pudding
Easy Apple Trifle
Apple Cheesecake
Apple Rice Pudding
Apple and Walnut Triangles
Toffee Apples
Apples in Toffee
Apple Cider Fruit Salad
Spiced Fruit Kebabs

APPLE ABERNETHY

125g, 5oz Abernethy or other plain biscuits, crushed
50g, 2oz (¼ cup) butter
small tin of condensed milk
1 egg, separated
juice of ½ a lemon
¼ tsp cinnamon
300ml, ½pt (1¼ cups) apple purée

Melt the butter and mix in the biscuit crumbs. Line a 20cm (8in) cake tin with this mixture. Whisk together condensed milk, egg yolk, cinnamon and lemon juice and mix in the apple purée. Whisk the egg white and fold it in. Pour mixture into the biscuit case. Bake in the oven at gas mark 4, 180°C (350°F) for about 30 minutes.

POLENTA CRUMBLE CAKE

Polenta is a maize-flour which is used extensively in Northern Italy and in Eastern Europe. It is now becoming widely available here. This recipe is delicious served hot with cream or cold and cut into slabs.

100g, 4oz (1 cup) polenta
225g, 8oz (2 cups) plain flour
1 tsp baking powder
125g, 5oz (¾ cup) caster sugar
rind and juice of ½ lemon
125g, 5oz (²/₃ cup) butter
1 egg
1 tbsp olive oil
450g, 1lb cooking apples, peeled, cored and sliced
75g, 3oz (½ cup) demerara sugar

Put the polenta, flour, baking powder and caster sugar in a food processor with the grated lemon rind. Process briefly and then add the butter and process until the mixture resembles fine breadcrumbs. Beat together the egg, 1 tablespoon of lemon juice and the oil and pour this into the processor while it is still running. Once everything is combined, press a little over half the mixture into a greased 22.5cm (9in) cake tin or pie dish. Mix the sliced apples with 50g, 2oz (¹/₃ cup) of the demerara sugar, add the remaining lemon juice and pile onto the base. Crumble the remaining pastry and and spread over the apples. Sprinkle the rest of the sugar over the top. Bake in the oven at gas mark 5, 190°C (375°F) for about 45 minutes or until golden brown.

APPLE CHARLOTTE

This is a classic pudding.

675g, 1½lb cooking apples, peeled, cored and sliced
100g, 4oz (²/₃ cup) caster sugar
rind and juice of 1 lemon
½ tsp cinnamon
50g, 2oz (¼ cup) melted butter
thin slices of brown or white bread (crusts removed)

Cook the apples with the rind and juice of the lemon, cinnamon, and 2 tablespoons of water until tender. Remove from the heat and mix in the sugar beating well. Meanwhile brush the melted butter all over the slices of bread and use them to line a soufflé dish. Pour in the apple purée. Cover with bread and bake in a reasonably hot oven at gas mark 6, 200°C (400°F) for about 30 minutes.

APPLE CHRISTMAS PUDDING

100g, 4oz (1 cup) breadcrumbs
50g, 2oz (½ cup) self-raising flour
50g, 2oz (½ cup) brown sugar
75g, 3oz (¾ cup) suet
100g, 4oz (²/₃ cup) seedless raisins
2 cooking apples, peeled, cored and grated
grated rind of 1 lemon
1 egg
3 tbsp milk

In a large mixing bowl first combine all the dry ingredients, then add the raisins, the grated apples, and the grated lemon rind. Stir thoroughly to combine everything well. Now beat the egg into the milk and stir into the mixture. Spoon into a greased 600ml (1pt) pudding basin, and cover the top tightly with greaseproof paper. Put a pleat in the paper to allow room for the pudding to rise. Secure with string. Steam the pudding in a steamer for 2 hours. Serve with brandy sauce, brandy butter or a custard.

GOOEY APPLE GINGERBREAD

This is an excellent log fire pudding or an alternative Christmas pudding.

Base

*3 Granny Smiths or other crisp eating apples, peeled,
cored and sliced
100g, 4oz (1 cup) brown sugar
50g, 2oz (¼ cup) butter*

Gingerbread

*100g, 4oz (1 cup) plain flour
½ tsp bicarbonate of soda
½ tsp ground nutmeg
1 tsp ground ginger
2 tsp cinnamon
pinch of ground cloves
1 egg
100g, 4oz (1 cup) soft brown sugar
3 tbsp black treacle
150ml, ¼pt (²/₃ cup) milk
50g, 2oz (¼ cup) melted butter*

To make the base, melt the butter and sugar together and spread it over the bottom of a 27.5 x 17.5cm (11 x 7in) rectangular ovenproof dish. Arrange the sliced apples on top of the brown sugar mixture. Sift the flour with the bicarbonate of soda and the spices, then mix in the egg, sugar, treacle, milk and melted butter and beat it until the mixture is smooth. Pour it over the apples and bake in the oven at gas mark 4, 180°C (350°F) for about 45 minutes. Serve with whipped cream.

APPLE AND LEMON
SURPRISE PUDDING

This is a yummy pudding. My children gave it 10/10.

450g, 1lb cooking apples peeled and cored
65g, 2½oz (¹/₃cup) butter
50g, 2oz (½ cup) brown sugar
100g, 4oz (²/₃ cup) granulated sugar
2 large eggs, separated
grated rind and juice of 1 large lemon
1 tbsp plain flour
150ml, ¼pt (²/₃cup) milk

Chop the apples into small pieces. Melt 50g, 2oz (¼ cup) of
the butter in a frying pan and stir in the apples and brown sugar.
Fry the apple pieces over a high heat, stirring all the time, for a
couple of minutes. Put in the bottom of a greased 20 x 15cm
cm (8 x 6in) rectangular pie tin. Beat the 15g, ½ oz (1 tbsp)
butter into the granulated sugar. Beat in the egg yolks, the lemon
rind and juice, the flour and milk. Whisk the egg whites and
gently fold into the lemon mixture. Pour this on top of the apples.
Stand the tin in another tin half full of cold water and bake in
the oven at gas mark 4, 180˚C (350˚F) for 30 minutes.

APPLE AND ORANGE PUDDING

450g, 1lb cooking apples, peeled, cored and sliced
1 tsp cinnamon
50g, 2oz (½ cup) soft brown sugar
25g, 1oz (2 tbsp) butter
grated rind and juice of a small orange
50g, 2oz (½ cup) fresh breadcrumbs
50g, 2oz (¹/₃ cup) caster sugar
1 small carton soured cream
3 large eggs, separated

Butter a 1.1litre (2pt) ovenproof dish. Arrange the sliced apples on the bottom of the dish and sprinkle with the cinnamon and brown sugar. Dot with the butter, and pour the orange juice over the apples. Put the breadcrumbs into a mixing bowl with the caster sugar, the soured cream, the egg yolks and the orange rind. Stir well together. Whisk the egg whites and fold them lightly into the yolk mixture. Pour on top of the apples and cook in the oven at gas mark 5, 190°C (375°F) for about 40 minutes.

OAT AND APPLE PUDDING

This is a definite favourite with children and is simple and quick to make.

1 large cooking apple, peeled and cored
2 tsp lemon juice
100g, 4oz (1¾ cups) porridge oats
50g, 2oz (½ cup) light brown sugar
25g, 1oz (2 tbsp) butter
double cream to serve

Fry the oats in the butter and, as they start to brown, add the sugar. Mix everything together and then allow to cool. Grate the apple and sprinkle with the lemon juice. Mix the apple into the oat mixture and serve with the cream immediately.

APPLE COBBLER

450g, 1lb cooking apples, peeled, cored and sliced
50g, 2oz (½ cup) brown sugar
1 tbsp orange juice
50g, 2oz (½ cup) stoned dates
2 bananas, sliced
1 tsp lemon juice

Topping

225g, 8oz (2 cups) plain flour
¼ tsp ground ginger
1 tsp bicarbonate of soda
1 tsp cream of tartar
50g, 2oz (¼ cup) margarine
150ml, ¼pt (²/₃ cup) milk
2 tbsp demerara sugar

Arrange the apples in a 20cm (8in) round ovenproof dish, sprinkle with the sugar and pour on the orange juice. Stir in the dates and cover the fruit with the bananas tossed in lemon juice. To make the topping, sift together the flour, ginger, bicarbonate of soda and cream of tartar and rub in the margarine until the mixture resembles breadcrumbs. Pour the milk into the dry ingredients, mix to a dough and knead until smooth. Roll the dough out to cover the apple mixture. Brush with milk and sprinkle with demerara sugar. Bake in the oven at gas mark 6, 200°C (400°F) for 20 minutes until the topping is well risen.

APPLE AND BLACKBERRY
AUTUMN PUDDING

This is a brilliant pudding to have in the autumn when you can
pick blackberries and apples are readily available.

1 sponge cake
450g, 1lb cooking apples, peeled, cored and sliced
675g, 1½lb blackberries
2 tbsp water
125g, 5oz (¾ cup) sugar
100g, 4oz (½ cup) cream cheese
150ml, ¼pt (²/₃ cup) single cream

Slice the sponge cake into three layers and put it in the bottom
of a greased 1.1litre (2pt) pudding basin and around the sides,
keeping a layer for the lid. Put the sliced apple with the blackberries in a saucepan with the water and sugar and simmer
until tender. Sieve the whole mixture. Mix the cream cheese
and cream and fold in the purée. Pour onto the sponge and top
with the lid. Place a plate on top with a weight on it and leave
overnight to allow the juices to soak into the sponge. Turn out
and serve straight away.

CHOCOLATE AND APPLE DESSERT

This dessert requires some effort but is ideal for a dinner party.

6 eggs, separated
225g, 8oz (1¹/₃ cup) caster sugar
275g, 10oz dark chocolate

Apple purée

900g, 2lb cooking apples, peeled, cored and chopped
1 tsp cinnamon
25g, 1oz (1tbsp) butter
300ml, ½pt (1¼ cup) double cream
100g, 4oz (1 cup) soft brown sugar
75g, 3oz (¾ cup) flaked almonds

Whisk the egg yolks in a bowl until thick, gradually adding the caster sugar. Break the chocolate into a bowl and melt over a pan of simmering water. Beat the melted chocolate into the egg yolk mixture. Whisk the egg whites until stiff and fold into the chocolate mixture using a metal spoon. Line two 30 x 25cm (12 x 10in) baking trays with greaseproof paper. Divide the chocolate mixture between the two trays and bake at gas mark 4, 180°C (350°F) for 20 - 25 minutes. Take them out of the oven, cover with a damp tea towel and leave to cool completely. Make the apple purée. Cook the apples with the cinnamon, butter and 4 tablespoons of water. Cook gently until soft and then allow to cool. Whip the cream with the brown sugar and fold into the apple. Spread half the apple mixture over one chocolate rectangle. Cover with the other one and spread the rest of the apple mixture on the top. Sprinkle with flaked almonds.

DAMSON AND APPLE OMELETTE

This is an unusual pudding but is quick and easy.

2 large eating apples, peeled, cored and sliced
225g, 8oz damsons, halved and stoned
15g, ½oz (1 tbsp) butter
50g, 2oz (¹/₃ cup) sugar
pinch of ground cloves
pinch of cinnamon
4 eggs, separated
3 tbsp soured cream

Put the apples, damsons and butter with half the sugar in a large frying pan. Cook over a gentle heat, until the fruit is softened, stirring all the time. Add the cloves and cinnamon and then remove from the heat. Beat the egg yolks with the cream and stir into the fruit. Whisk the egg whites until stiff and fold them in. Cook over a low heat until the mixture sets. Sprinkle the top with sugar and brown under a hot grill. Serve immediately.

APPLE PROFITEROLES

Makes 16 profiteroles

These are made with choux pastry and filled with stewed
apple and cream.

Pastry
50g, 2oz (¼ cup) butter
65g, 2½oz (⅔ cup) plain flour
2 eggs, beaten
150ml, ¼pt (⅔ cup) water

Filling
450g, 1lb cooking apples, peeled cored and sliced
50g, 2oz (⅓ cup) sugar
150ml, ¼pt (⅔ cup) double cream
icing sugar

Put the water and the butter into a saucepan. Heat slowly until
the butter melts, then bring to the boil. Lower the heat and tip
in all the flour and salt at once. Stir rapidly until the mixture
forms a soft ball and leaves the sides of the pan. Leave to cool
slightly. Gradually add the eggs, a little at a time, beating until
the mixture is smooth and shiny. Spoon 16 balls of the mixture
on to a buttered baking sheet. Bake the profiteroles at gas
mark 6, 200°C (400°F) for 10 minutes. Remove from the oven
and make a slit in the side of each and then return to the oven
for a further 5 minutes. Cool on a wire rack. For the filling,
cook the apple with the sugar and 2 tablespoons of water until
soft. Fold the stewed apple into whipped cream. Fill the
profiteroles with the apple mixture and dust with icing sugar.

APPLE SOUFFLÉ

Apple base

900g, 2lb cooking apples, peeled, cored and sliced
75g, 3oz (⅓ cup) butter
100g, 4oz (1 cup) brown sugar

Soufflé

50g, 2oz (¼ cup) butter
50g, 2oz (½ cup) flour
450ml, ¾pt (1¾ cups) milk
150ml, ¼pt (⅔ cup) Calvados or brandy
50g, 2oz (⅓ cup) caster sugar
5 eggs, separated

Butter and dust a soufflé dish with a little caster sugar. Melt the butter for the apple base and dissolve the brown sugar in it. Boil for a few minutes. Add the apples and cook for about 5 minutes. Pour into the soufflé dish. For the soufflé, melt the butter in a saucepan and stir in the flour. Gradually add the milk, stirring all the time. Let the sauce boil. Then take the saucepan off the heat and stir in the Calvados or brandy. Beat in the sugar and then the yolks one by one. Whisk the egg whites until stiff, and with a large metal spoon, fold them into the sauce quickly and thoroughly. Pour the mixture over the apples and bake in the oven at gas mark 7, 220°C (450°F) for 40 minutes. Serve straight away.

BAKED APPLES

1 large cooking apple for each person
a little brown sugar
a knob of butter
a little golden syrup

Wash the apples well, remove the centres with a corer and make a cut in the skin round the middle of the apple. Place in a buttered ovenproof dish. In the hole in the centre of each apple place a teaspoon of brown sugar, a knob of butter and fill up with golden syrup. Bake in the oven at gas mark 6, 200°C (400°F) for about 45 minutes.

APPLE MERINGUES

2 egg whites
100g, 4oz (²/₃ cup) caster sugar
325g, 12oz eating apples, peeled, cored and thinly sliced
50g, 2oz (½ cup) brown sugar
Greek yoghurt, or whipped cream

Whisk the egg whites until stiff. Add half the caster sugar and whisk again. Fold in the remaining sugar. Spoon rounds of meringue mixture on a baking sheet and bake at gas mark 1, 120°C (275°F) for about 2 hours. Put the apples, sugar and 2 tablespoons of water in a saucepan. Cover and cook gently for about 10 minutes. Cool and chill. Sandwich the meringues together with a spoonful of the stewed apple mixed with a spoon of yoghurt, or cream.

GOLDEN APPLE PUDDING

450g, 1lb cooking apples, peeled and cored
grated rind and juice of 1 lemon
50g, 2oz (½ cup) brown breadcrumbs
25g, 1oz (1 tbsp) butter, melted
125g, 5oz (¾ cup) caster sugar
2 eggs, separated

Grate the apples into a bowl. Stir in the lemon rind and juice, breadcrumbs, melted butter, 75g, 3oz (½ cup) of the caster sugar and the egg yolks. Mix well together. Whisk the egg whites until stiff. Whisk in the remaining 50g, 2oz ($^1/_3$ cup) of sugar and then whisk this meringue mixture into the apple mixture. Turn into an ovenproof dish and bake in the oven at gas mark 4, 180°C (350°F) for 45 minutes. Serve hot with cream.

EASY APPLE TRIFLE

300ml, ½pt (1¼ cups) sweetened apple purée
2 tbsp blackberry jelly
225g, 8oz sponge cake
150ml, ¼pt ($^2/_3$ cup) ready-made custard
150ml, ¼pt ($^2/_3$ cup) whipped cream

Layer the bottom of a dish with slices of sponge cake. Top with the apple purée, allowing juices to soak into the sponge. Spread the blackberry jelly over the apple. On top of this pour the custard. Finish by covering with freshly whipped cream.

APPLE CHEESECAKE

450g, 1lb cooking apples, peeled, cored and sliced
100g, 4oz (½ cup) butter
¼ tsp mixed spice
¼ tsp cinnamon
75g, 3oz (½ cup) caster sugar
1½ tsp gelatine or vege-gel (the vegetarian equivalent)
juice of ½ lemon
125g, 5oz (1¼ cups) ginger biscuits, crushed
225g, 8oz (1 cup) cream cheese
1 egg white
150ml, ¼pt (²⁄₃ cup) double cream

Stir the lemon juice into the gelatine or vege-gel. Leave to swell. Cook the apples gently with 50g, 2oz (¼ cup) of the butter, mixed spice, cinnamon and sugar. Then stir in the gelatine or vege-gel mixture to dissolve. Sieve the apple mixture. Melt the remaining butter, stir in the crushed biscuits and spread this mixture in a 20cm (8in) flan dish to cover the bottom and sides. Soften the cheese and beat in the cooled apple mixture. Whisk the egg white and whip the cream. Fold both into the apple mixture and spread evenly over the biscuit base. Chill until set. You can decorate the cheesecake with slices of eating apples brushed with lemon juice to prevent them from turning brown.

APPLE RICE PUDDING

This pudding is popular with the whole family.

100g, 4oz (½ cup) pudding rice
300ml, ½pt (1¼ cup) milk
225g, 8oz (1¹/₃ cup) sugar
grated rind of 1 lemon
2 eggs, separated
675g, 1½lb cooking apples, cored, peeled, and sliced
25g, 1oz (2 tbsp) butter
150ml, ¼pt (²/₃ cup) apple juice

Put the milk and lemon rind in a saucepan with the rice. Bring to the boil and then turn the heat right down, cover and simmer for 10 minutes. Mix in 2 tablespoons of the sugar and the egg yolks. Put half the rice mixture in a baking dish. Cover with half the apples, sprinkle with 2 tablespoons of sugar and dot with half the butter. Cover with the rest of the rice and then the remaining apples, 2 more tablespoons of sugar and the remaining butter. Pour the apple juice over the apples and bake in the oven at gas mark 3, 160°C (325°F) for 45 minutes. Beat the egg whites in a bowl and fold in the last 2 tablespoons of sugar. Spread the meringue over the apple and return to the oven for about 20 minutes until the meringue is golden brown.

APPLE AND WALNUT TRIANGLES

Shortbread

75g, 3oz ($^1/_3$ cup) butter
50g, 2oz (½ cup) soft brown sugar
100g, 4oz (1 cup) plain flour
75g, 3oz (¾ cup) walnuts, crushed

Filling

1 tbsp apricot jam
450g, 1lb eating apples, peeled, cored and sliced
½ tsp cinnamon
150ml, ¼pt ($^2/_3$ cup) whipped cream

Cream the butter and sugar together until light and fluffy. Stir in the flour and walnuts and mix to a firm dough. Turn out on a floury surface and knead until smooth. Roll the dough out and cut into triangles. Place on a greased baking tray and bake in the oven at gas mark 4, 180°C (350°F) for about 12 minutes. Cool on a wire rack. Place the jam and apples in a pan, cover and cook gently until soft. If you find the apple is sticking to the bottom of the pan add a little water. Add the cinnamon and cool. Spread the apple mixture over the triangles and top with spoonfuls of cream.

TOFFEE APPLES

Makes 8 toffee apples

8 good eating apples
325g, 12oz (2 cups) demerara sugar
40g, 1½oz (3 tbsp) butter
1 tsp vinegar
90ml, 3fl oz (¹/₃ cup) water
1 tbsp golden syrup

Push a skewer into the core of each apple. Heat all the other ingredients gently in a saucepan until the sugar has dissolved. Then boil for 5 minutes without stirring until a little mixture dropped into cold water forms a hard ball. Remove from the heat and dip the pan into cold water at once to stop the cooking. Dip the apples into the mixture and twirl around until evenly coated. Place on an oiled baking sheet until the toffee has hardened.

APPLES IN TOFFEE

A simple quick pudding for the children.

4-5 cooking apples, peeled, cored and sliced
1 tbsp butter
2 tbsp golden syrup
1 tbsp sugar
juice of ½ lemon

Put the butter in a frying pan and allow to melt over a low heat. Add the golden syrup and sugar and heat gently, stirring. Add sliced apples and the lemon juice and cook until the sauce becomes more toffee like and the apples are soft.

APPLE CIDER FRUIT SALAD

600ml, 1pt (2½ cups) sweet cider
75g, 3oz (½ cup) caster sugar
juice of 1 lemon
150g, 6oz black grapes
150g, 6oz white grapes
2 eating apples, cored
225g, 8oz strawberries
2 peaches
2 bananas

Put the cider in a saucepan and boil rapidly for 10 minutes to reduce the liquid. Stir in the sugar and lemon juice and leave to cool. Prepare the fruit. Halve and deseed the grapes, chop up the apples, slice the peaches and bananas and hull the strawberries. Mix all the fruit except the bananas with the cider syrup. Stir in the bananas just before serving.

SPICED FRUIT KEBABS

Makes 8 kebabs

2 oranges
2 red-skinned eating apples, cored, such as Laxtons or
Spartans
2 bananas
16 pineapple chunks
100g, 4oz (½ cup) butter
2 tbsp sugar
1 tsp mixed spice

Slice the oranges. Cut the apples into quarters. Cut the bananas into 4 pieces. Thread alternate pieces of fruit including the pineapple chunks onto skewers. Melt the butter in a saucepan. Stir in the sugar and spice. Put the skewers on a barbecue grill or on a grill pan under a hot grill. Brush with the spicy butter and cook basting frequently and turning so all sides brown.

Apple Loaf

Apple and Cider Bread

Apple Scones

Apple and Bran Muffins

Apple and Blackberry Muffins

Apple Flapjack

Apple and Cinnamon Slices

Apple Shortbread

Fruity Shortbread

Cider Cake

Easy Apple Cake

Guernsey Apple Cake

Chocolate Apple Cake

Apple Gingerbread

Cream Cheese Apple Slices

APPLE LOAF

Makes 1 loaf

50g, 2oz (¼ cup) soft margarine
50g, 2oz (½ cup) brown sugar
1 egg, beaten
100g, 4oz (1 cup) plain wholemeal flour
100g, 4oz (1 cup) breadcrumbs
1½ tsp baking powder
½ tsp cinnamon
½ tsp ground mixed spice
½ tsp nutmeg
450g, 1lb Cox's eating apples, peeled, cored and sliced
2 tbsp apple juice

Cream the margarine and sugar together. Gradually add the beaten egg. Fold in the flour, breadcrumbs, baking powder and spices and then mix in the apple slices and apple juice. Transfer the mixture to a greased 450g (1lb) loaf tin and bake in a pre-heated oven at gas mark 4, 180˚C (350˚F) for 1 hour. Cool on a wire rack. Slice and eat with butter.

APPLE AND CIDER BREAD

Makes 2 loaves

50g, 2oz dried apple rings
450ml, ¾pt (1¾ cups) cider
1 sachet quick acting yeast
4 tbsp warm water
450g, 1lb (4 cups) wholemeal flour
1 tsp salt

Put the apple rings in a saucepan with the cider. Bring to the boil and cook gently for about 5 minutes until the apple has softened slightly. Leave to cool and measure out 300ml, ½pt (1¼ cups) of liquid - some will have evaporated. Put the flour in a bowl, add the yeast. Then add the warm water and apple liquid. Mix to a dough and knead for at least 5 minutes. Cover with a damp tea towel and leave to double in size in a warm place for about an hour. Punch down the dough. Divide in half and put into two 675g (1½lb) loaf tins. Cover and leave to rise again. Bake in the oven at gas mark 6, 200°C (400°F) for about 25 minutes.

APPLE SCONES

Makes 12 scones

225g, 8oz (2 cups) plain flour
2 tsp baking powder
50g, 2oz (¼ cup) margarine
50g, 2oz (¹/₃ cup) caster sugar
3 apples (eaters or cookers) peeled, cored and grated
4 tbsp milk

Sieve together flour and baking powder. Rub in margarine and add sugar, apple and enough milk to make a soft dough. Knead lightly and roll out. Divide into rounds. Place on greased baking sheets. Brush with milk and a little sugar and bake at gas mark 6, 200°C (400°F) for 20 minutes. Turn out and cool a little on a wire rack. Serve with butter and jam.

APPLE AND BRAN
MUFFINS

Makes 12 muffins

50g, 2oz (¼ cup) margarine
75g, 3oz (¾ cup) muscovado sugar
2 tbsp black treacle
2 eggs, beaten
240ml, 8fl oz (1 cup) milk
150g, 6oz (1½ cups) plain flour
1½ tsp baking powder
½ tsp bicarbonate of soda
½ tsp salt
65g, 2½oz (1²/₃ cups) natural bran
75g, 3oz (½ cup) raisins (optional)
1 large eating apple, peeled cored and chopped

Cream the margarine with the sugar and beat in the treacle.
Add the eggs and milk. Sift the flour, baking powder,
bicarbonate of soda and salt together and add the bran. Pour
the wet ingredients on to the dry ones and add the raisins and
apple. Stir and then divide the mixture into 12 greased deep
muffin tins and bake at gas mark 6, 200°C (400°F) for 20
minutes until well risen and brown. Serve warm with butter
and jam or honey.

**APPLE AND BLACKBERRY
MUFFINS**

Makes 12 muffins

*225g, 8oz (2 cups) plain flour
1 tsp bicarbonate of soda
240ml, 8fl oz (1 cup) yoghurt
120ml, 4 fl oz (½ cup) sunflower oil
1 egg
1 tsp vanilla essence
2 Cox's apples, peeled and grated
12 tsp of blackberry jelly*

Sift the flour and bicarbonate of soda together. Beat together the yoghurt, oil, egg, grated apple and vanilla essence. Mix the flour into this mixture. Place a spoonful of batter into each compartment of a greased muffin tin. Add the teaspoon of jam and then cover with more batter. Bake in the oven at gas mark 6, 200°C (400°F) for 20 minutes. Serve warm.

APPLE FLAPJACK

450g, 1lb cooking apples, peeled, cored and sliced
100g, 4oz ($^2/_3$ cup) sugar
125g, 5oz ($^2/_3$ cup) butter
4 tbsp golden syrup
225g, 8oz (3 cups) porridge oats
1 tsp ground ginger

Simmer the apples gently in a covered pan with 75g, 3oz (½ cup) sugar, until soft. Cool slightly. Heat the remaining sugar with the butter and syrup until dissolved. Stir in the oats and ginger. Line the base of a greased 27.5 x 17.5cm (11 x 7in) baking tin with three-quarters of the flapjack mixture. Pour the apple purée over it and cover with the remaining mixture, pressing it down. Bake at gas mark 5, 190°C (375°F) for 30 minutes. Allow to cool before cutting into slices. Serve dusted with some icing sugar.

APPLE AND CINNAMON SLICES

These slices have a flapjack like texture and are really quite
delicious. My children love them.

125g, 5oz (1¼ cups) self-raising flour
150g, 6oz (2¹/₃ cups) porridge oats
175g, 7oz (1¾ cups) soft brown sugar
2 tsp ground cinnamon
175g, 7oz (¾ cup) margarine, melted
2 medium cooking apples, peeled, cored and sliced

Combine flour, oats, sugar, and cinnamon. Then add melted
margarine and mix thoroughly. Put half the mixture into a greased
27.5 x 17.5cm (11 x 7in) baking tin and press down. Cover
with sliced apples and then with the rest of the mixture. It may
be quite difficult to spread this on top of the apples. Bake in
the oven at gas mark 4, 180°C (350°F) for 25 minutes. Allow
to cool before cutting into slices.

165

APPLE SHORTBREAD

150g, 6oz (1½ cups) plain flour
100g, 4oz (½ cup) butter
50g, 2oz (½ cup) soft brown sugar
1 large cooking apple, peeled and cored
4 tsp demerara sugar
¼ tsp ground cinnamon
2 tsp ground almonds

Put the flour in a bowl, add the butter cut into small pieces, together with the brown sugar. Rub in the butter until the mixture resembles fine breadcrumbs, then knead until the mixture leaves the sides of the bowl clean. Turn onto a lightly floured surface. Knead until the dough is smooth and silky and then roll out to a 20cm (8in) round on a greased baking sheet. Slice the apple thinly and arrange on top of the shortbread, leaving a border. Mix the demerara sugar, cinnamon and almonds and sprinkle over the apples. Bake in the oven at gas mark 4, 180°C (350°F) for about 30 minutes or until the shortbread is golden brown at the edges and the apple tender. Serve warm cut into slices.

FRUITY SHORTBREAD

225g, 8oz (2 cups) wholemeal flour
2 tsp baking powder
pinch of salt
100g, 4oz (½ cup) butter
75g, 3oz (¾ cup) soft brown sugar
1 egg, beaten
2 eating apples, peeled, cored and sliced
2 bananas, sliced
325g, 12oz cottage cheese, sieved
50g, 2oz (½ cup) soft brown sugar
15g, ½oz (1 tbsp) butter

Mix together the flour, baking powder and salt. Rub in the butter and stir in the brown sugar. Mix to a soft dough with the beaten egg. Roll out and line a greased Swiss roll tin with the pastry. Spread the apple and banana over the pastry and top with the cottage cheese. Sprinkle with the brown sugar and dot with butter. Bake in the oven at gas mark 5, 190°C (375°F) for 35-40 minutes. Cool and cut into squares.

CIDER CAKE

150ml, ¼pt (²/₃ cup) dry cider
225g, 8oz (1¹/₃ cups) sultanas
100g, 4oz (½ cup) butter
100g, 4oz (1cup) light soft brown sugar
2 eggs, beaten
225g, 8oz (2 cups) plain flour
1 tsp bicarbonate of soda

Put the cider and sultanas in a bowl and leave to soak overnight. Cream the butter and sugar together. Gradually beat in the eggs. Add half the flour and the bicarbonate of soda and beat thoroughly. Pour over the sultanas and the cider and mix well. Fold in the remaining flour and pour into a greased 20cm (8in) square cake tin. Bake at gas mark 4, 180°C (350°F) for about 1 hour. Leave to cool in the tin. Turn out and cut into squares.

EASY APPLE CAKE

150g, 6oz (¾ cup) butter or margarine
150g, 6oz (1 cup) caster sugar
3 eggs, beaten
1 tsp cinnamon
½ tsp mixed spices
150g, 6oz (1½ cups) self-raising flour
300ml, ½pt (1¼ cups) apple purée
1 tbsp demerara sugar

Grease a 22.5 x 17.5cm (9 x 7in) baking tin. Beat the butter or margarine and caster sugar together. Then add the beaten eggs a little at a time. Sift the spices and flour together and add to the mixture alternating with the apple purée. Pour into the baking tin, sprinkle with the demerara sugar and cook at gas mark 4, 180°C (350°F) for 25 minutes. Serve hot straight from the tin as a pudding with cream, or allow to cool, cut into squares and serve at tea-time.

GUERNSEY APPLE CAKE

This is a solid but quite moist cake which can be eaten in one's fingers. It's a good cake for a picnic lunch.

225g, 8oz cooking apples, peeled, cored and sliced
juice of ½ lemon
225g, 8oz (2 cups) plain wholemeal flour
100g, 4oz (½ cup) butter
150g, 6oz (1 cup) demerara sugar
2 large eggs, beaten
1 tsp ground nutmeg
1 tsp cinnamon

Toss the apple in the lemon juice, then add the flour. Mix them well together, cover and leave for at least 1 hour. Cream butter and sugar and mix in the eggs a little at a time. Add the spices to the flour and apple mixture and mix into the butter, sugar and eggs. Grease a 20cm (8in) cake tin and spoon in the cake mixture. Bake in the oven at gas mark 3, 160°C (325°F) for 1 hour. Take out and cool before serving.

CHOCOLATE APPLE CAKE

The chocolate and apple pieces in this cake make a delicious
combination of flavours.

250g, 9oz (2¼ cups) self-raising flour
25g, 1oz (1 tbsp) cocoa powder
1 tsp baking powder
1 tsp bicarbonate of soda
100g, 4oz (½ cup) butter
250g, 9oz (1½ cups) caster sugar
2 eggs
a few drops of vanilla essence
150ml, ¼pt (²/₃ cup) milk
2 cooking apples, peeled, cored and finely chopped

Icing
450g, 1lb (2¾ cups) icing sugar, sifted
25g, 1oz (1 tbsp) cocoa powder
50g, 2oz (¼ cup) butter
90ml, 3fl oz (¹/₃ cup) milk

Beat together the butter and sugar. Whisk in the eggs, one at a
time and add the vanilla essence. Sift together the flour, cocoa
powder, baking powder and bicarbonate of soda and add a
little of the flour mixture alternately with the milk until you have
mixed in all the flour and milk. Add the chopped apples. Spoon
into a greased 20cm (8in) square cake tin and bake at gas
mark 4, 180°C (350°F) for 45 minutes or until a skewer stuck
into the cake comes out clean. Turn out onto a wire rack and
leave to cool. For the icing, mix together icing sugar, cocoa,
butter and milk. Whisk until smooth. Spread on the top and
sides of the cake.

APPLE GINGERBREAD

This is a simple gingerbread with grated apple in it.

125g, 5oz (1¼ cups) light brown sugar
50g, 2oz (2 tbsp) golden syrup
100g, 4oz (4 tbsp) black treacle
150g, 6oz (¾ cup) margarine
1 large cooking apple, unpeeled and grated
150g, 6oz (1½ cups) self-raising flour
3 tsp ground ginger
2 eggs, beaten

Heat the sugar, syrup and treacle together with the margarine. Sift the flour with the ginger. Add the beaten eggs and melted mixture to the flour and beat until smooth. Stir in the grated apple and spoon into a greased 27.5 x 17.5cm (11 x 7in) baking tin. Cook in the oven at gas mark 4, 180°C (350°F) for about 1 hour or until a skewer comes out clean. Cool in the tin before cutting up and sieve with icing sugar before serving.

CREAM CHEESE APPLE SLICES

Pastry base

150g, 6oz (1½ cups) plain flour
½ tsp baking powder
½ tsp cinnamon
¼ tsp ground cloves
¼ tsp ground ginger
25g, 1oz (¼ cup) brown sugar
100g, 4oz (½ cup) butter
1 tbsp sherry
2 tbsp milk

Filling

2 large cooking apples, peeled, cored and sliced thinly
225g, 8oz (1 cup) cream cheese
75g, 3oz (½ cup) sugar
3 eggs
1 large can of condensed milk
juice and grated rind of ½ lemon
½ tsp vanilla essence
1 tbsp flour

For the pastry, sift the dry ingredients and add the butter, rubbing it in gently with your finger tips. Add the sherry and milk and blend into a dough. Roll out and line a greased 20cm (8in) square baking tin. For the filling, place the apple slices over the pastry base. Beat together the cream cheese, sugar, and eggs. Add the condensed milk, lemon juice, rind, vanilla and sifted flour. Pour this mixture over the apples and bake in the oven at gas mark 4, 180°C (350°F) for 30 minutes.

JAMS AND JELLIES

Blackberry and Apple Jelly

Crab-Apple Jelly

Mint and Apple Jelly

Redcurrant and Apple Jelly

Apple Marmalade

Apple and Pear Cheese

Rose-Hip and Apple Cheese

Apple Lemon Curd

BLACKBERRY AND APPLE JELLY

Makes about 4kg (9lb)

1kg, 2.4lb cooking apples peeled, cored and sliced
1kg, 2.4lb blackberries
water
preserving sugar

Cook the blackberries and apples together with enough water to just cover the fruit. When soft pour into muslin and suspend over a large bowl. Allow to drip through the muslin over night and squeeze as much liquid out of the muslin as you can the next day so that you are left with just a mush of blackberry pips. Pour the blackberry and apple liquid into a large saucepan and add the sugar. For every 600ml or 1pt of juice you need 450g, 1lb of sugar. Boil rapidly until set. You can test for a set by dropping a little of the hot liquid onto a saucer. If it appears jelly-like then remove immediately from the heat. Have several jars warmed and ready and carefully pour the hot jelly into them. Seal well.

CRAB-APPLE JELLY

Makes about 4kg (9lb)

This jelly is delicious with pork or roast goose.

2kg, 4½lb crab-apples
preserving sugar
juice of 1 lemon

Roughly chop the apples without peeling them. Put them into a large saucepan and cover with water. Simmer until the apples are soft. Pour into a jelly or muslin bag and strain the juice into a large bowl. Measure out the juice and add the sugar. For every 600ml, 1pt (2½ cups) of juice add 450g, 1lb *(2²/₃ cups)* of sugar. Return to the saucepan, add the lemon juice and boil rapidly for about 10 or 15 minutes until setting point is reached. Pot and cover.

MINT AND APPLE JELLY

Makes about 5½ kg (12 lb)

This version of apple jelly goes particularly well with roast lamb.

2.7kg, 6lb cooking apples, washed and roughly chopped
600ml, 1pt (2 ½ cups) white wine vinegar
juice of 4 lemons
1 litre, 1¾pts (4 cups) water
1 bunch of fresh mint and 3 tbsp finely chopped mint
granulated or preserving sugar

Put the apples into a preserving pan and add the vinegar, lemon juice and enough water just to cover. Add the bunch of mint. Bring to the boil and simmer for about 1 hour. Beat to a purée and sieve. Measure the juice and add 450g, 1lb *(2²/₃ cups)* of sugar per 600ml, 1pt (2½ cups) of juice. Heat until the sugar is dissolved then boil rapidly until setting point is reached. Skim and stir in the chopped mint. Pour into warmed jars and seal well.

REDCURRANT AND APPLE JELLY

Makes about 4½ kg (10lb)

This jelly goes well with roast lamb or lamb chops.

900g, 2lb redcurrants
1.4kg, 3lb cooking apples, cored and chopped
1 litre, 1¾pts (4 cups) water
granulated or preserving sugar

Put the redcurrants and apples in a large saucepan or preserving pan and add the water. Bring to the boil and then simmer for about 1 hour. Beat well and put the mixture through a sieve. Measure the juice and add 450g, 1lb (2⅔ cups) of sugar per 600ml, 1pt (2½ cups) of juice. Heat until the sugar dissolves and then boil rapidly until setting point is reached. Pour into warmed jars and seal.

APPLE MARMALADE

Makes about 4kg (9lb)

This is also known as apple butter. It can be used as a
spread or makes an excellent filling for tarts or cakes.

600ml, 1pt (2½ cups) cider
granulated sugar
2kg, 4½lb cooking apples peeled, cored and quartered
rind and juice of 1 lemon
2 tsp cinnamon
1 tsp ground cloves
mixed spice

Put the quartered apples and the cider in a large saucepan and
bring to the boil. Simmer uncovered until the apples are mushy
and then rub through a fine sieve. For every 600ml, 1pt (2½
cups) of apple liquid add 450g, 1lb (2⅔ cups) of sugar. Return
the apple and sugar mixture to the saucepan and add the
cinnamon, cloves, mixed spice, lemon rind and juice. Stir over
a low heat until the sugar has dissolved. Bring to the boil and
boil until setting point is reached. Pour into jars and seal well.

APPLE AND PEAR CHEESE

Makes about 1.4kg (3lb)

Fruit cheeses are very thick preserves which can be potted in moulds or jars and turned out whole. These cheeses keep very well. This is delicious eaten with bread and dairy cheese, or you can also serve it with meat.

675g, 1½lb cooking apples, cored, and chopped
675g, 1½lb pears, cored and chopped
juice of 1 lemon
pinch of ground nutmeg
sugar .

Put the fruit in a heavy saucepan and half cover with water. Cover and simmer until very soft and pulpy. Press the fruit through a sieve to make a smooth purée. Weigh the purée and return to a cleaned pan with lemon juice and nutmeg. Simmer until thick. Stir in the sugar until it dissolves. For every 450g, 1lb apple purée allow 450g, 1lb (2²/₃ cups) of sugar. Cook gently for about 1 hour. The mixture must be thick. Pour the fruit cheese into a mould or jars.

ROSE-HIP AND APPLE CHEESE

Makes 1.4kg (3lb)

This is an unusual fruit cheese and delicious served with
meat or on bread or toast.

900g, 2lb cooking apples
50g, 2oz rose-hips
300ml, ½pt (1¼ cups) orange juice
150ml, ¼pt (²/₃ cups) water
granulated sugar

Wash and chop the unpeeled and uncored apples. Slice the
rose-hips and place them in a muslin bag. Put the apples and
rose-hips in a preserving pan with the orange juice and water.
Cook over a gentle heat until the apples are soft. Discard the
muslin bag of rose-hips. Sieve the apples and weigh the purée.
For every 450g, 1lb apple purée allow 450g, 1lb (2²/₃ cups)
of sugar. Return to the saucepan and simmer for at least 1 hour
until very thick. Stir frequently to prevent the mixture sticking
to the bottom of the pan. Spoon into jars and seal well.

APPLE LEMON CURD

Makes about 900g (2lb)

This makes a good filling for sponge cakes or for tarts.

900g, 2lb cooking apples, peeled, cored and chopped
225g, 8oz (1¹/₃ cups) sugar
225g, 8oz (1 cup) butter, melted
2 eggs
juice of 1 lemon

Cook the apple in a little water until soft and then beat to a purée. Add sugar and melted butter and beat in the eggs. Cook the mixture slowly in a bowl over a pan of simmering water for about 30 minutes. When it is thick, add the lemon juice. Pour into jars and seal well.

MICROWAVE APPLE PUDDINGS

Here are some basic apple puddings that you can have ready in a few minutes by using a microwave. Sometimes I'm in a tremendous rush but need to do a pudding for three hungry children. You can have these simple apple recipes prepared and ready within a matter of minutes.

Apple and Oat Layer

Apple Crumble

Baked Apples

Eve's Pudding

APPLE AND OAT LAYER

100g, 4oz (½ cup) butter or margarine
50g, 2oz (½ cup) light brown sugar
2 tbsp golden syrup
225g, 8oz (3½ cups) oats
1 large cooking apple, peeled, cored and sliced
1 tsp cinnamon

Place the butter, sugar and syrup in a bowl. Microwave on high power for 1-2 minutes or until melted. Stir in the oats. Spread half the oat mixture into a microwave dish. Arrange the apples over the top in overlapping rows and sprinkle with cinnamon. Gently press the remaining oat mixture over the apples. Microwave for 6 - 8 minutes or until the mixture is firm and golden brown. Cut into slices while hot and then allow to cool in the dish.

APPLE CRUMBLE

675g, 1½lb cooking apples, peeled, cored and sliced .
150g, 6oz (1 cup) demerara sugar
100g, 4oz (½ cup) butter or margarine
150g, 6oz (1½ cups) plain wholemeal flour
½ tsp cinnamon

Place apple slices in dish, sprinkle with 75g, 3oz (½ cup) of the sugar. Cover and microwave for 3 minutes until the apples just begin to soften. Rub the margarine into the flour and cinnamon until mixture resembles breadcrumbs. Stir in remaining sugar. Sprinkle the crumble over the apples to cover the fruit. Microwave for 6-8 minutes or until golden brown and crisp.

BAKED APPLES

2 large cooking apples
rind of 1 lemon and 2 tbsp lemon juice
75g, 3oz (¹/₃ cup) butter
50g, 2oz (½ cup) flour
½ tsp cinnamon
50g, 2oz (¾ cup) muesli
2 tbsp brown sugar

Cut the apples in half, remove core and place in dish. There is no need to peel the apples. Fill each centre with the lemon juice and rind. Rub butter into flour and cinnamon, add muesli, and sugar. Lightly press the mixture onto the apples and microwave for 6-7 minutes or until the apple is soft.

EVE'S PUDDING

450g, 1lb apples, peeled, cored and sliced
1 tbsp caster sugar
juice of ½ lemon
100g, 4oz (²/₃ cup) caster sugar
100g, 4oz (½ cup) margarine
2 eggs, beaten
100g, 4oz (1 cup) self-raising flour
1 tbsp milk

Put apple slices in a dish and sprinkle over sugar and lemon juice. Cover and microwave for 2 minutes. Drain apples. Cream together the sugar and margarine, add eggs and fold in the flour. Mix to a stiff consistency with the milk. Spread the mixture over the apples. Smooth the top with a spoon and microwave for 6-8 minutes or until golden brown.

DRINKS

Apple Fizz

Apple Punch

Cider Making

Wittenham Cider

Mulled Cider

APPLE FIZZ

3 eating apples, cored and sliced
2 tsp lemon juice
1 part Pimm's
1 part apple juice
2 parts lemonade

Sprinkle the apple slices with lemon juice to prevent them going brown. Put into a jug and pour over the Pimm's and apple juice and then add the lemonade.

APPLE PUNCH

8 lemon tea bags
1 bay leaf
8 cloves
1 cinnamon stick
1 litre, 1¾pts (3²/₃ cups) boiling water
50g, 2oz (¼ cup) soft brown sugar
1½ litre, 2½pts (6 cups) apple juice
600ml, 1pt (2½ cups) ginger ale

Put the lemon tea bags into a bowl or large jug with the bay leaf, cloves and cinnamon stick, and pour on the boiling water. Leave to infuse for 30 minutes. Remove the tea bags. Stir in the brown sugar and allow to cool. Pour the tea into a large punch bowl and add the apple juice and ginger ale. Add ice just before serving and garnish with lemon wedges.

CIDER MAKING

Cider apples are grown in the South West of England - varieties include Kingston Black, Foxwhelp, Crimson King and Langworthy. If only non-cider apples are available then use Worcester Pearmains, Cox's Orange Pippins or Russets. Unlike soft fruits apples must be minced or crushed and then pressed before the pure juice can be extracted.

The following recipe is for real cider made from the pure juice from apples. You will need access to a fruit press so you may want to buy one. Small fruit presses are sold by home-brew stockists.

To make 5 litres (just over a gallon) of real cider you will need about 9kg (20lb) of apples and the apples should be a mixture of sweet and bitter apples.

Other ingredients

1 tbsp of strong brewed tea
1 tbsp lemon juice
an all purpose wine yeast starter bottle

Wash the apples and cut out any nasty bits. Chop the apples but do not remove the skins, cores or pips. Extract the juice with your fruit press, and let the juice run into a sterilised, plastic, food grade bucket. Add the tea and lemon juice to the bucket and then cover. Add the activated wine yeast from your starter bottle. Check that you have enough space at the top of your bucket to allow for frothing and foaming. Keep somewhere warm for 5 days and stir juice a couple of times a day. After 5 days, strain into a sterilised narrow-necked glass or plastic vessel. Fit a sterilised, rinsed bored cork or rubber bung and an air lock filled with water to the neck or plug the neck with cotton wool or polythene smoothed tightly over the top of the vessel and secured with an elastic band. Keep the cider like this until it has finished fermenting - this will probably take between 12 and 17 days. If you have fitted an air lock you will know the fermenting has finished because there will be no more bubbles of carbon dioxide gas showing. If you have fitted cotton wool or polythene, watch the surface of the cider and make sure that all bubbles have stopped.

To double check that fermenting has finished pour a little cider into a glass and taste it. If it tastes dry and there is no fizz then you are ready for the next stage.

Syphon the cider back into your bucket and cover. Rinse out the sediment from the vessel and sterilise it again. Pour the cider back into the vessel through a funnel. Top up to the neck with water. Plug the neck again with the cork or rubber bung (not the cotton wool). Cover the bung with some polythene smoothed over it and secured with elastic bands to guard against the bung flying off, due to any small fermentation occurring.

Now you need to store your cider in a cool place for 4 months to clear and mature.

When the 4 months are up the cider will be ready for bottling.

You will need to use special home-brew beer bottles and bottle caps. Ordinary bottles and caps may not be able to stand the high pressure of carbon dioxide gas which may develop in your home-made cider.

Remember to sterilise all your equipment again. Stand your vessel on a surface higher than the bucket. Use a syphon and put one end in the cider so it rests above the sediment. Suck some cider into the tube and place in your bucket. The cider should flow into the bucket.

At this stage you have to decide whether you want sparkling or still cider.

For still cider: Use a sterilised jug to pour cider from your bucket and pour through a polythene funnel into your sterilised home brew bottles. You can use plastic caps on the bottles for still cider.

For sparkling cider: For every 4½ litres (1 gallon) of cider, pour a few cupfuls of cider into a saucepan and heat until simmering. Then dissolve 2 tablespoons of honey or 1½ tablespoons of granulated sugar into it. Cover and allow to cool.

Pour the sweetened cider back into the bucket with the rest of the cider. Stir well and leave for at least 10 minutes to blend. Fill your home-brew bottles as you did for the still cider but use metal caps and a capping tool to crimp the edges of the metal cap securely around the mouth of the bottles and make the seal air-tight.

WITTENHAM CIDER

This is an easy-to-make old fashioned apple drink.

1.4kg, 3lb cooking apples
900g, 2lb (5¹/₃ cups) sugar
grated rind and juice of 3 lemons
7 litres, 12 pts (30 cups) water

Wash the apples and cut out any nasty bits. You do not need to peel or core the apples. Chop them up and put them through a mincer. Then put them in a large earthenware or plastic pan and pour on the water. Leave them for a week, stirring them well twice a day. Then strain off the liquid and into this stir the sugar and grated rind and juice of the lemons. Leave for another whole day and then strain and bottle in screw-topped bottles. (The tops must be the type to withstand fermentation gas pressure). The cider will be ready to drink after a week but tastes even better if left for a few months.

MULLED CIDER

6 cloves
1 litre, 1¾pts (3²/₃ cups) cider
1 cinnamon stick
2 tsp ground ginger
50g, 2oz (½ cup) brown sugar
150ml, ¼pt (²/₃ cup) water
1 small orange, peeled and sliced
1 eating apple, cored and sliced

Heat the cider gently in a saucepan. Put the cloves, cinnamon stick, ginger, sugar and water in another saucepan and stir over a gentle heat until the sugar has dissolved. Simmer gently for a few minutes. Pour the hot cider, the strained spicy water and the sliced orange and apple into a large punch bowl. Give the mulled cider a stir and serve.